Luther on Worship

An Interpretation

Luther on Worship

by Vilmos Vajta

Wipf and Stock Publishers
199 W 8th Ave, Suite 3
Eugene, OR 97401

Luther on Worship
An Interpretation
By Vajta, Vilmos

ISBN: 1-59752-031-4
Publication date 12/22/2004
Previously published by Muhlenberg Press, 1958

CONTENTS

Introduction ix

Principles of Worship

1. Worship and Idolatry 3
2. Beneficium and Sacrificium 27

Worship as the Work of God

3. The Proclamation of the Word 67
4. The Presence of Christ in the Lord's Supper 85
5. The Office of the Ministry as Impartation of the Gift of God 109

Worship as the Work of Faith

6. Faith and Worship 125
7. The Priestly Sacrifice of Believers 149
8. Faith (Freedom) and Love (Order) in Worship 171

Bibliography 191

Index 195

Note on footnotes and bibliography: All references to foreign language periodicals can be found in the original German work, *Die Theologie des Gottesdienstes bei Luther.* References marked *WA* are to volume and page of the Weimar edition of *Luther's Works:* TR refers to Table Talk, Bibel to the Bible volumes, and Br to Luther's correspondence.

INTRODUCTION

What is worship?

Lately, this question has come increasingly to the fore. A quest for liturgical reform has been awakened in many churches and lands.[1] And worship has become a significant topic of ecumenical conversation.[2] But the problem involved is not simply one of liturgical orders and forms, for worship and theology belong together. Through the history of the church worship and doctrine have developed in mutual dependence.[3] The his-

[1] A liturgical renaissance has been evident since the time of the First World War: cf. Gustav Mensching, *Die liturgische Bewegung in der evangelischen Kirche* (Tuebingen: 1925), and *Katholische Kultprobleme* (Gotha: 1927). While these early trends towards a liturgical renewal were often motivated by purely esthetic considerations, the period between the two wars has been marked by a deeper theological interest; cf. Rudolph Staehlin, "Die Geschichte des christlichen Gottesdienstes von der Urkirche bis zur Gegenwart," *Leiturgia,* I, 1 (Kassel: 1952), p. 74ff, and (concerning the development in the Roman Catholic church) *Liturgische Erneuerung in aller Welt,* ed. by Th. Boegler (1950); E. B. Koenker, *Liturgical Renaissance in the Roman Catholic Church* (Chicago: Univ. of Chicago Press, 1954).

[2] The question of worship forms one of the main themes for the study groups of the ecumenical movement; cf. the Reports of the Lund Conference of 1952; "Ways of Worship," ed. P. Edwall, E. Hayman, W. D. Maxwell (1951), and "Intercommunion," ed. D. Baillie and J. Marsh (1952).

[3] Peter Brunner states: "There is no area in the life of the church where the formative power of the confession is more clearly evident than the order of worship. It is not only significant that certain creeds form part of the liturgy, but the whole liturgy represents an actualized confession. Liturgy is dogma prayed and confessed. The dogmatical decisions of the church become concrete in her liturgy and in this way have caused divisions as well as mergers in the church." "Die Ordnung des Gottesdienstes an Sonn- und Feiertagen" in *Der Gottesdienst an Sonn- und Feiertagen* (Guetersloh: 1949), p. 10. Cf. also the works of Franz S. Renz, Darwell Stone, and Yngve Brilioth, and Paul Graff, *Geschichte der Aufloesung der alten gottesdienstlichen Formen in der evangelischen Kirche Deutschlands,* I—II (Goettingen: 1921-39).

tory of Christian worship reflects the confessional struggles of every age, as well as the theological differences within denominations. One need only point to the connection between the Roman mass and medieval theology or to the fatal relation of the decline of worship to certain theological trends in Protestantism.

This link between worship and theology is most evident at the great watershed of the Reformation. Luther could not avoid coming to grips with the mass. The liturgical reforms which he touched off were the direct outgrowth of his rediscovery of the gospel. His newly found theological convictions led to a complete liturgical reorientation. It is therefore not enough to examine the actual liturgical reforms introduced by Luther and his collaborators. The inner motives for these reforms must be explored and set within the framework of his whole theology. On the whole, this task has been neglected by the older literature on Luther's liturgics. His theology of worship was taken as a matter of course, and scholars asked only how his own practical proposals as well as modern liturgical trends might be evaluated from these premises.[4] The danger of this approach is obvious. Generally accepted "truths" are apt to become theologically meaningless and, if left unchallenged, they become dangerous half-truths. One of these half-truths is the current as-

[4] Among works of this type we would mention Karl Holl, "Was koennen wir fuer die Neugestaltung unseres evangelischen Gottesdienstes von Luther lernen?" in *Gesammelte Aufsaetze zur Kirchengeschichte*, III (Tuebingen: 1928); Friedrich Flemming, *Die triebenden Kraefte in der lutherischen Gottesdienstreform* (Leipzig: 1926); Luther D. Reed, *The Lutheran Liturgy* (Philadelphia: 1947); P. Z. Strodach, Introduction to Vol. VI of *The Works of Martin Luther* (Philadelphia: Holman, 1915). The advantage of a more systematic study of Luther's theology of worship is in the unbiased approach which we will be able to follow. Instead of beginning with the problems of the liturgical movement, we will be able to set forth Luther's views from the center of his theology. Thus free play will be given Luther in developing both the questions and the answers.

sumption that Luther had been liturgically uninterested.[5] From a merely historical viewpoint, his liturgical output may indeed appear meager and inadequate. And would-be liturgical reformers are always inclined to bypass the Reformation as they ransack the liturgical treasure chambers of the past. But their liturgical interest begins where it should end, *viz.* at the question of liturgical forms. Often they pay scant attention to the theology which underlies these forms and accept from other sources materials which are quite inconsistent with the teachings of the Reformation.

Luther's preoccupation with the doctrine of "justification by faith" has often been blamed for his alleged liturgical indifference. But recent research has been able to trace his theology of worship right down to this basic conviction.[6] Nevertheless, a systematic presentation of Luther's theology of worship is still wanting. This is the task which we have set ourselves. We would like to clarify the inner connection between Luther's theology as a whole and his theology of worship. But rather than follow the gradual emergence of his views,[7] we shall try to present them in systematic order. The question of the "young Luther" can be left out of our discussion, for his general theological convictions were quite settled and mature when he was forced to take a stand with respect to worship. Of course, in liturgical details he changed his mind occasionally, without affecting his principal views on the meaning of worship.

In the course of this inquiry we will have to link Luther's

[5] See for example F. Flemming, *op. cit.*, p. 45f; Einar Molland, *Luthers liturgiske intensjoner* (Oslo: 1938), p. 126. R. Staehlin (*op. cit.*, p. 60) views the liturgical significance of Luther even more critically: "We shall have to admit Luther's limitations in the liturgical field. Luther neither realized the theological meaning of liturgical structure nor the unfolding of redemptive action in the liturgical act." Our study leads us to different results.

[6] Cf. O. Dietz, *op. cit.*, p. 30ff.

[7] This development has been traced by A. Allwohn, *op. cit.*

theology of worship with his teaching on creation, the atonement, the church, and justification. If proof of this connection can be established—and we mean to furnish it—it follows that Luther's theology of worship points to the very center of his whole thought. This would confirm the experience of many Luther scholars that a study of Luther leads one into the center of the Christian faith whatever one's point of departure may be.

Our study, while centering on the public communion service (the mass), aims to clarify Luther's total view of worship.

Luther's theology of worship is deeply significant for the theological and liturgical problems of our day. Of course it does not offer an answer to every liturgical question or a panacea for all our liturgical ills. But it deserves the attention of all who are concerned with the renewal and reform of worship in the Lutheran church of our day. We cannot hope to master these problems unless we have been confronted with Luther. His insights into the meaning of worship are significant not only for the Lutheran church but, beyond denominational boundaries, for ecumenical conversation on the meaning of worship.

Luther on Worship

PRINCIPLES OF WORSHIP

1

Worship and Idolatry

"The words 'I am thy God' are the standard and measure of everything that can be said about worship."[1] These words of Luther show that God and worship belong together. A person's picture of God determines his idea of worship. Indeed, the First Commandment is basic for Luther's idea of worship. Faith itself is the essence of worship; for faith is the fulfilment of the First Commandment,[2] and idolatry is nothing but unbelief.[3] Man must decide between worship and idolatry. There is no other choice.[4] Either God is "our God," and we live in fellowship with him, or else by distrust despise him. The one implies worship, the other idolatry.

Thus the problem of worship hinges on two questions: Who is the God who speaks to us in the First Commandment? And how should that commandment be fulfilled? Luther's answer is determined by the fact that he sees God as the one who acts for us. He is our God on account of his deeds for us. As he proved himself the God of Israel by the exodus and other mighty signs, so has he acted for us by sending Christ into the world. Christ died and rose *for us*. He is *our* God,[5] for he still acts for *us* in the Word, Baptism, and the Lord's Supper. The foundation of wor-

[1] *WA* 18, 69; cf. 7, 595 and 10 I, 1, 533.
[2] *WA* 6, 212; 10 I, 1, 684.
[3] *WA* 6, 210; 28, 574 (Roerer).
[4] *WA* 28, 590 (Roerer).
[5] Cf. *WA* 16, 424ff.

ship is in the command to receive these blessings by faith. The First Commandment requires faith; without faith we cannot serve God and render acceptable worship to him.

God and Faith

"What is it to have a god? or what is God?"[6] This is Luther's classical formulation of the problem of God in the Large Catechism. The very form of the question is significant. By equating the question "What is it to *have* a god?" with "What *is* God?" Luther shows that the God whom he seeks and whom he hears in the Decalogue is one who establishes fellowship with man, *i.e.* the God of revelation ("thy God"). The quest for the essence of God is the quest for fellowship with him. Man cannot seek God as a spectator who looks on from afar. He asks for God because he has been totally shaken by the call from that God who is uncomfortably near and close to him.

In answer to his own question, Luther explains: "To have a god is to trust and believe him from the whole heart, as I have often said that the confidence and faith of the heart alone make both God and an idol (*Gott und Abegott*). If your faith and trust be right, then is your god also true. On the other hand, if your trust be false and wrong, then you have not the true God; for these two belong together, *viz.* faith and God. That now, I say, upon which you set your heart and put your trust, is properly your god."[7]

Here it must be noted that Luther is wont to use the terms "god" and "faith" in a twofold meaning. In the wider sense, they include both the true God and false gods, both true and false faith. But properly speaking, they refer only to the true

[6] *WA* 30 I, 132. English translation by H. E. Jacobs, *The Book of Concord* (Philadelphia: United Lutheran Publication House, 1911), p. 391.
[7] *WA* 30 I, 133; English translation by H. E. Jacobs, *op. cit.*, p. 391.

God and the true faith respectively. This ambiguity must be remembered in the interpretation of the paragraph which we quoted.

The crucial passage in Luther's reply is this: "The confidence and faith of the heart alone make both God and an idol." Not that Luther intended to "psychologize" the concept of God or to make God a creation of the human mind.[8] To make man the creator of God would be to misinterpret Luther. The context shows that the faith of a man may be directed in one of two directions, either towards the Creator, the Giver of every good and perfect gift, or towards created things. In this sense, faith, right or wrong, makes a decision, as it directs itself either to that God who says to man: "I am thy God" or to an idol, a non-god. Luther never doubted that man as such must come to this decision as he directs his faith either in this or that direction; for he is so created that he must believe. He is made for fellowship with God. By "making both God and an idol" he confirms his humanity. The fact that man cannot escape the one or the other proves the reality of God's creatorship. God is not a creature of man; man is a creature of God. This relatedness to God indicates the reality of his fellowship with God. Thus faith whether right or wrong is related to the Creator. For the faith which clings to idols functions according to its created destiny, although the perversity of man corrupts the actualization of his trust.

Luther's "faith and confidence of the heart" are thus not the spontaneous quest of the human heart for a distant god. To him God is present in his creation through the very law which forces man to trust and believe. Faith and God are correlative. One cannot speak of the one without implying something of

[8] Feuerbach's misinterpretation of this passage comes from disregarding the fact that according to Luther only the god of false religion should be regarded as *phantasma.*

the other.[9] God and man cannot be isolated in Luther's thought. God is what he is as, in wrath or love, he acts with and for man. Man is what he is as, by faith or unbelief, he meets his God.[10] Luther is not concerned with the modern antithesis of religion versus atheism; for to him man lives always in "commerce" with God. This can be either the true communion where he believes and trusts the Creator, or a false one where he puts faith in the created things of this earth.[11]

Faith cannot be neutral. It is no empty concept, but always filled, either by God or by an idol. But in either case, the true God is at work. In Luther's theology, this can be shown both from the relation between God and idols, and from the concept of faith as it emerges in a more detailed examination of the relation of the Christian faith to Christ.

The name and power of the true God is hidden even in idols.[12] Religion is universal,[13] because this world was created by God. Every man and every nation must produce a concept of God. Man's sin stamps these ideas with his disobedience, but the compulsion by which he produces idols stems from his depend-

[9] *WA* 56, 234.

[10] Cf. F. Gogarten, *Die Verkuendigung Jesu Christi* (Heidelberg: 1948), pp. 305 and 325. The neutral consideration of man *an sich* belongs to philosophical anthropology; cf. esp. *Disputatio de homine, WA* 39 I, 175ff. More in G. Ljunggren, *Synd och skuld i Luthers teologi* (Stockholm: 1928), p. 54ff.

[11] *WA* 56, 13: "For man's mind is by nature so unsteady that when it turns from the one, it must by necessity turn to something else. Therefore when it turns from the Creator, it will by necessity turn to the creature." This explains the "dualistic" approach of Luther; cf. G. Wingren, *Luther on Vocation* (Philadelphia: Muhlenberg, 1957), p. 93ff. For Luther, atheism is impossible, for it is self-deception; cf. H. Olsson, *Grundproblemet i Luthers socialetik* (Lund: 1934), I, p. 36.

[12] *WA* 19, 404: "God protects his name so rigidly that not even in the idols will he allow it to be blasphemed, since all the idols claim the name of 'god' and are so called." Cf. H. Bornkamm, *Luther und das Alte Testament* (Tuebingen: 1948), p. 41ff.

[13] *WA* 30 I, 134: "For there has never been a nation so wicked as not to establish and hold some sort of worship."

ence on God. Even the heathen's idolatry bears witness to the true God. Reason indeed knows the concept of an omnipotent god and helper in need,[14] but this knowledge is perverted in the cult of idols and man-made gods which belong to creation themselves.[15]

This reference to the role of reason must not be misunderstood to mean that man's reason is able to develop a formal concept of God and had erred only in its content. Man has been made to believe and trust in a god. Even idolatry betrays the destiny of man. Idolatry does not equal "godlessness," and the idolater does not cease to be in relation to God. Of course, the idols are empty and vain. But their power to call forth awe, worship, and obedience comes from God. It is his wrath which subjects men to the figments of their own making. And those who worship idols meet the true God in his wrath. Therefore God will punish even those who mock or despise the idols, for in the idols the true God confronts them.[16]

All this goes to show that Luther's concept of God is far from abstract. His question is not whether or not man ought to have a god but rather whether he worships God or an idol. The problem of God is not a theoretical one which can be decided at leisure, for man is always either for or against the true God.

Luther's concept of faith agrees with these views. Here too the question is not whether or not man ought to believe, for man is always and ever a believer. Either he believes in created things or in Christ. But faith in Christ is not an act of man, not even a capacity of man, but is Christ himself coming to man.[17]

[14] *WA* 19, 206.
[15] *WA* 56, 177.
[16] *WA* 19, 404.
[17] *WA* 40 I, 546, 545. This thought has been thoroughly expounded by Regin Prenter, *Spiritus Creator* (Philadelphia: Muhlenberg, 1953), pp. 27-64.

He comes, not to fill a vacuum, but to fight, vanquish, and dethrone the idols. In him the purpose of creation is fulfilled. God the Creator and Giver of life rules through Christ and the gospel. The scholastics spoke of the *habitus* (the habitual attitude) infused into man's soul by divine grace. Faith was to them a *qualitas haerens in corde, excluso Christo* (a quality inherent in the heart, even apart from Christ), and so a rather static condition.[18] But Luther's concept of faith is more dynamic. According to him, Christian faith cannot exist unless Christ himself continues to come, to fight, and to vanquish.[19]

The ambiguity of the terms "god," "faith," and "confidence" derives from Luther's understanding of creation and the law on the one side, and atonement through Christ (the gospel) on the other side. As idols are not unrelated to God, so unbelief and trust in idols are related to true faith and confidence. That is why they are sometimes comprehended under the terms "God," "faith," and "confidence" which are ordinarily restricted to the specifically Christian usage. The apparent contradiction is expressive of the paradoxical nature of the Christian message. God fights the devil although he vanquished him long ago and obtained the victory.[20]

The foregoing discussion will have thrown light on the statement, "The confidence and faith of the heart alone make both God and idol." Luther's view combines both God, dealing with man through gospel and law, in love or in wrath, and man, bound to believe and trust, bowing before God or an idol. There

[18] *WA* 40 I, 545.

[19] *WA* 40 I, 228: "In faith itself Christ is present."

[20] When we use the term "dualistic," it is to be understood, not in a metaphysical sense (as in the dualism of mind versus matter), but in the meaning of a struggle between God and the devil. This is the meaning in which the term has been used by Swedish theology where it was coined by Gustaf Aulén and extensively explained in Ragnar Bring's monograph: *Dualismen hos Luther* (Lund: 1929).

is a law of creation which compels man to have and to make his gods. And as long as he is under the devil's dominion he must create his gods in the image of his own desires. The idols of the heathen world were brought forth by man's desire for fortune in war, fertility, health, beauty, etc.[21] And essentially the same desires have led to the adoration of the saints under the papacy, for the different saints were supposed to serve every selfish want and wish of man.[22]

Man, estranged from God, is bound to create a profusion of idols. Idolatry is a companion of work righteousness, the desire to influence God by certain works of our own. In this connection Luther pointed to the monks as being makers of gods (*fabricatores deorum*).[23] Says he, they have become the victims of their own sinful imagination. But they will not escape the God of the law who meets such perversion with the full severity of the law.

The same thought crops up again in his explanation of Romans 1 where he connects God's wrath with man's deification of the creature.[24] Of course, when men "changed the glory of the incorruptible God into an image" (Rom. 1:23), they could effect no change in the actual essence of God. What they changed was their concept of God.[25] The reference to man as maker of gods implies no dependence by God on the imagination of men. Man cannot oppose or exalt himself over God in his real essence (*in substantia sua*). God in his majesty remains unaffected by the rantings and fancies of men. But it is possible for man to exalt himself above the God who deals with him through preaching and worship. For here he is the God who suffers and is despised—the God of the cross.[26]

[21] *WA* 30 I, 135; 28, 609.

[22] *WA* 1, 425; 28, 610.

[23] *WA* 13, 229.

[24] *WA* 56, 11ff and 174ff.

[25] *WA* 56, 12.

[26] *WA* 18, 658.

In the First Commandment, God speaks as "*my* God." Luther always connected the First Commandment with faith in Christ. Fallen man indeed "has" idols. But he cannot properly call them "*his* gods"; for more truly, they are his foes. Only by faith in Christ do we know God as "*our* God." In this context, Luther also called the Christian faith a maker of God (*Gottmacher*), but in a very different sense from the one noted above, for this faith accepts God as he comes to us, and not as fancied by men. In Christ, we meet God as the one who is not "for-himself," but "for-us." Only through him do we come to know the one who says, "I am the Lord thy God." These words reveal to us the God of the gospel. Properly speaking it is only faith in Christ which "has God," for here God is on our side. He comes into our need as a Saviour and gives himself "for us." Christ is God for us (*Deus pro nobis*) and our God (*Deus noster*).

This discussion may help to elucidate some of Luther's favorite sayings which otherwise are apt to be misunderstood. Take the dictum *Glaubst du, so hast du, glaubst du nicht, so hast du nicht*[27] (To believe is to have; not to believe is not to have). This, of course, does not refer to God in his majesty. You won't escape him by your lack of faith. On the contrary you are totally under his wrath. But "having the God of the law" is tantamount to not having God at all, for God's mercy and love are the heart of his being. On the other hand, it is faith in Christ by which we come to know God as he really is; for it is his will and eternal resolve to allow himself to be found only in Christ. And as he is in Christ, so is he in his very nature and essence. There is no contradiction between the God of faith and revelation and the

[27] *WA* 2, 719; 18, 769; 33, 132; 5, 578; 7, 24; 1, 595; 27, 402 (Roerer); 40 I, 444, and the Sermon on Matthew 8:13, "As thou hast believed, so be it done unto thee," in 37, 451ff. Luther's protest against the *opus operatum* and his stress on the *opus operantis* (2, 751) must also be explained on the basis of the creative power of faith.

eternal, unchangeable, "hidden" God.[28] Luther can therefore say that faith is a "creator of God" and "perfects the godhead," i.e. in us.[29]

In this context we must remember what was said about the connection between our faith and our concept of God. The love of God and his wrath are related to faith in Christ or to the lack of it and are really the expression thereof. Luther speaks of the changeableness of God as being tied up with the believing attitude (*Glaubenshaltung*) of man. God's wrath and his love, as it were, are prompted by the faith or unbelief of man.[30] Faith could almost be said to have the power of transforming God. But it must be observed that these references to the transforming power of faith do not mean to imply that man could control God. In the last analysis, our relation to God depends on God in his real essence (*Deus in substantia sua*) or God hidden in the way he predestines (*Deus absconditus in praedestinatione*), for faith is not without God. God dwells in it either as love or as wrath.[31]

We may summarize our findings as follows: Luther solves the problem of the nature of God by describing the nature of fellowship with God. The latter is a relation with God, determined by God himself who through faith dwells in man. The dualism in

[28] This identity between the "hidden" and the "revealed" God has been stressed by Ferdinand Kattenbusch in "Deus absconditus bei Luther," *Festgabe fuer J. Kaftan* (Tuebingen: 1920), especially pp. 183, 197, 205. Cf. Emanuel Hirsch, *Luthers Gottesanschauung* (Goettingen: 1918), p. 28.

[29] *WA* 40 I, 360.

[30] *WA* 14, 607 (V); 608 (D) and 13, 228.

[31] Reinhold Seeberg, "Die Lehre Luthers," *Lehrbuch der Dogmengeschichte* (Leipzig: 1917), IV:1, on pp. 47, and 175f; and Erich Seeberg, *Grundzüge der Theologie Luthers* (Stuttgart: 1940), on pp. 49f, 126f, 143, and 216 call this transforming power of faith "religious transcendentalism." This connects Luther's theology with the philosophy of Immanuel Kant, but overlooks the dualistic emphasis and the interest in redemptive history characteristic of Luther's theology.

God (wrath versus love, law versus gospel) corresponds with the dual nature of fellowship with God (unbelief versus faith); for faith implies fellowship with God. This correspondence between faith and God allows Luther to define man's fellowship with God on the basis of faith without forsaking his theocentric approach or getting lost in psychological categories. For in Luther's whole thought, the centrality of faith implies the centrality of God.

Worship as Fellowship with God

At this point it may seem as if we have lost sight of our original goal of describing the relationship between the worship of God and the picture of God in Luther's thought. Actually, this is not so, for Luther thinks of worship when he speaks of God and faith.

The words *fides* (faith), *religio* (religion), and *cultus* (worship) are used synonymously in his writings.[32] In the Large Catechism he proceeds naturally from the question of faith and God to the problem of worship, for to him worship is fellowship with God by faith. Faith does not belong to a province in the inner soul of man, but is realized in worship. Thus the antithesis "worship versus idolatry" is only a variation of the other antithesis "God (faith) versus idol (unbelief)." Everything that we have said thus far applies to our theme: Luther's concept of worship.

Worship is inherent in the created nature of man. As man must form a concept of God, so he must worship. Faith breathes worship. Fallen man has not only a false faith and a false confidence in idols, but also false worship. Unbelief results in idolatry. Idolatry is unbelief in action.[33]

[32] Cf. Herbert Vossberg, *Luthers Kritik aller Religion* (Leipzig-Erlangen: 1922), pp. 14ff., 22.

[33] *WA* 56, 178f.

Man is not free to choose his cult. Even Adam in paradise was given his altar, the tree of which God's command spoke to him.[34] And since the fall, man has become a maker of gods who worships the figments of his own making. Such idolatry, while proving man's perversion, is really an indication of the fact that he belongs to God; for it is a caricature of his natural relation to God. Luther would call even idolatry a sort of worship, a cult proving that man belongs to the true God. As we found an element of faith in the very unbelief of man, so we find an element of worship in idolatry.[35] Luther was led to this conclusion, not by a formal idea of worship which could be filled with differing concepts, either Christian or non-Christian, but by his dualistic-dramatic concept of God. He was able to detect the worship of God, though terribly corrupted, even in the hypocrisy of the Pharisees, the perversions of Israel, and the abominations of the heathen.[36] But he also pointed out that men who worship gods of their own making are led to pride and to the presumption that God could be reconciled by their works.[37] Their worship is under the wrath of God. Idolatry belongs with unbelief, with the devil, and with work righteousness, and is therefore diametrically opposed to faith in Christ.[38] In unbelief, it is the devil who "rides" man and makes him bow to the idols. Similarly, faith is warfare under the leadership of Christ. It is no static attitude, but a very active thing. True faith implies works.

[34] *WA* 42, 72.

[35] *WA* 38, 586.

[36] *WA* 25, 257; 31 II, 278.

[37] *WA* 25, 502: "For where faith is lacking, it follows at once that [people expect to become righteous] by their works. And where that happens, the true God is no longer present, but Baal Peor, he who is terrible, who . . . claims satisfaction from us. Thus they have preached God. Thus God is preached by all who are outside the Christian faith." Cf. 38, 587.

[38] *WA* 10 I, 1, 684; cf. TR 5, 198.

And worship is the battleground where the works of the devil are destroyed.

Christ lives in the believer and acts through him, even as the devil dwells and works through the unbeliever. Man has no free will. He is under authority, either God's or the devil's. Worship and idolatry are faith and unbelief in action, for neither faith nor unbelief are ever dormant or idle. They encompass all of man's life. This is the reason why Luther applied the idea of worship to every phase and province of life.[39] He included daily work under the term "worship" and called the monkish disdain of secular callings "idolatry." To love the neighbor and so to obey the Lord is worship. But any attempt to serve God other than as he wants to be served, is idolatry.[40]

As worship and faith are synonymous, so also God and worship are mutually related. In *De Servo Arbitrio* (*On the Bondage of the Will*) Luther distinguishes between the revealed God and the hidden God. Only the God who revealed himself in Christ is *our* God. It is he who wants to deal with us. Luther calls the revealed God (*Deus revelatus*) also the God who is preached (*Deus praedicatus*) and the God who is worshiped (*Deus cultus*). The God revealed is the God of pulpit and altar. Not the God who is hidden in eternal majesty and glory, but the God who is revealed is adored.[41] As the God who is worshiped, God is clothed in the earthly media of the Word, of Baptism, and of the Lord's Supper, wherein he reveals himself.[42] For only here is Christ

[39] Karl Holl, *Gesammelte Aufsaetze*, I, p. 105ff and Adolph Allwohn, "Das Wort Gottes und die Predigt," in *Stromata* (Leipzig: 1930), p. 133f.

[40] *WA* 10 I, 1, 674.

[41] *WA* 18, 685: "It is one thing to speak of God or of that will of God which has been proclaimed, revealed, offered, and worshiped. And it is another to speak of God as he is not proclaimed, revealed, offered, or worshiped. As far as God hides himself and prefers to remain unknown to us, he does not concern us."

[42] *WA* 25, 127.

present and active. By revealing himself in Christ, God himself instituted a definite form of worship. In the incarnation he humbled himself to meet us on the earthly level and clothed his gift to us in earthly forms. Thus there can be no fellowship between God and man except through the means of grace which belong to God's revelation in Christ.[43]

Thus worship is based on the very nature of man's fellowship with God. It is in the incarnate Christ that this fellowship is realized. Worship is an expression of the fact that God is not "naked God" (*Deus nudus,* i.e. God in his absolute essence and majesty), but a God who is worshiped and clothed in human form *(Deus cultus, involutus in humanitate).* This view rules out any and all spiritualizing ideas of worship. God revealed meets us through externals. And to meet him thus is worship.

Therefore whenever Luther speaks of God, he speaks also of worship. Worship is inseparable from the God who revealed himself in Christ. It is much more than a form of response to God. That would imply a certain freedom on the part of man, as though man were independent of God and could decide at leisure whether or not he wanted to have any sort of worship. But worship is given whenever we speak of God. Revelation and worship constitute one and the same reality: fellowship between God and man on the earthly level.

We are now ready to answer the question of how the ideas of the God who is preached and the God who is worshiped are related. Certainly these are not opposing concepts. They stand side by side and are used more closely to define the terms *Deus revelatus* and *Deus oblatus* (the revealed God and the God who offered himself). Their function is to indicate the respective ways and means by which God reveals and offers himself.

[43] *WA* 18, 689; TR 1, 467.

The co-ordination of these two terms is not by chance. Elsewhere Luther speaks of God revealing himself through his "work and word" (*opus et verbum*).[44] God's Word interprets his work. God's activity in the created world becomes evident to men through the Word. His Word opens our eyes to the works of God which are done all around us. There is no competition between Word and work; one depends on the other. God reveals himself through both Word *and* work, because he himself became true man and assumed manhood in Christ.

As Word and work belong together, so do preaching (*praedicatio*) and worship (*cultus*). Conditioned by God's mode of revelation, they form an organic unity. But a distinction remains in that God's works can never take the place of his Word; and his Word becomes empty apart from the works of God to which it points.[45]

This relation between preaching and worship has been misconstrued in two ways. Some theologians assume a contrast bebetween the two and would eliminate the element of worship as inconsistent with a "spiritual" understanding of religion. Such is the Neo-Protestant depreciation of the Sacrament and its subordination to the Word. Karl Holl interprets Luther's views in this manner. The Reformer did not make the sacrament subordinate to the Word, nor the Word to sacrament. He co-ordinated them.[46]

[44] *WA* 23, 189.

[45] Cf. below the chapter on The Proclamation of the Word, p. 67. Cf. also Helmut Gollwitzer, *Luthers Abendmahlslehre* (Muenchen: 1938), p. 115f.

[46] Allwohn has shown that Holl misunderstood the passages on which he based his argument. Regin Prenter, in *Spiritus Creator,* has pointed out that we are faced with an instance of loose terminology in the Psalm commentaries of the young Luther and that the whole trend of the work points rather to a co-ordination of Word and sacrament. This would correspond to the co-ordination of word (*verbum*) and sign (*signum*) in Luther's early writings.

It is therefore not correct to speak of a "dissolution of formal worship,"[47] of "noncultic" worship,[48] or of a "de-culting" (*Entkultung*) of worship[49] with reference to Luther. The true worship of faith is by no means incompatible with the "external things" of the cult.[50] The cult must be seen as a means of revelation, sanctioned by God himself. Of course, if by "cult" we mean the attempt of man to maintain himself before God, we start from false premises. Luther certainly would have rejected a cult which raised such pretensions.[51] But that is not to restrict worship to the sole task of providing suitable forms for mutual edification.[52] Worship is an ordinance of God, for God acts through externals.

Other theologians deprecate the Word, and would dissociate the service from the sermon. But to Luther, the sermon is more than talking about the acts of God. It is God's revelatory activity. Cultic acts belong to the warfare between God and the devil. It is the devil's influence which leads man to the presumption that he could be justified by good works. This is the view of religion as a human work effective by its mere performance (*opus operatum*) which is the archenemy of the Christian faith. And this presumption can be nullified only by the preaching of the Word. For the sermon resists the self-exaltation of man who

[47] Georg Rietschel, *Lehrbuch der Liturgik* (Berlin: 1900), I, p. 23f.

[48] F. Flemming, *Die treibenden Kraefte*, p. 29ff.

[49] Goetz Harbsmeier, "Das Problem des Kultischen im evangelischen Gottesdienst," *Bultman-Festschrift* (Stuttgart-Köln: 1949), especially p. 108f.

[50] The ambiguity in Rietschel's discussion of this problem results from the fact that he cannot find the connection between the worship of faith and love and the worship of the congregation. It persists also in his *Lehrbuch der Liturgik*, I, p. 30. On the whole it would seem that students of Luther have dwelt on his critical remarks about liturgical ceremonies with a somewhat stubborn one-sidedness in order to prove Luther's alleged reservations about worship. Rietschel and Flemming in *Die treibenden Kraefte*, p. 26f. both quote passages on ceremonies, fasting, etc. But these certainly are not of the essence of worship!

[51] G. Harbsmeier, *op. cit.* p. 100. [52] *Ibid.*, p. 123f.

would use even the ordinances of God for his self-justification. The God who is preached and the God who is worshiped is one in his revelation. Thus the works of God cannot be divorced from his Word.

This leads us to Luther's so-called "critique of religion"[53]; for the latter implies also a "critique of worship." As the Christian faith stands apart from every other religious faith, so Christian worship, as instituted by Christ, stands over against every human attempt to serve God. The heathen and the papists, the Jews and the Turks are examples of idolatry.[54] All these stand outside of the Word and the divine institution of worship, and invent their own form and mode of worship.[55] But every form of man-made worship is idolatry and nothing more.

We may now summarize our findings for the total aspect of Luther's theology of worship. Luther developed his theology of worship along two lines, as he proceeded either from his picture of God or from his concept of faith. God and faith belong together. They are not opposing ideas, but form an essential unity. The strength of Luther's theology lies in his keeping both of them equally in view.

He followed the meaning of worship either along the line of the picture of God or along the line of the idea of faith. At one time he described God's gifts through Word and sacraments, at another he showed how faith rests on these. But both lines formed a necessary unity in the description of fellowship with God. When this unity is destroyed worship becomes idolatry, the love of God wrath, and faith unbelief. This unity also marks the ideas of God and faith.

[53] Cf. for this the study by Herbert Vossberg.

[54] In H. Vossberg, *Luthers Kritik aller Religion,* p. 97, note 4; p. 100, note 3; and p. 114f, a number of relevant Luther passages are quoted.

[55] *WA* 19, 206; 25, 128.

1. God revealed himself in Christ in order to establish fellowship with mankind, to lead them to worship or to make them his worshipers. This revelation, incarnation, or condescension of God takes place through the means of grace. The God of worship who reveals himself in the Word and the sacraments is God-for-us (*Deus pro nobis*). To ignore this reference to mankind would be to misunderstand worship completely. The incarnation is connected with the idea of God and therefore also that of worship. Here is the foundation for a faith that will accept God as he gives himself.

2. Faith is more than a human faculty to be described in psychological terms, more than the quest of man for a God who is far away and high above. If this were so, faith would depend on the degree of "spirituality" in the individual. But faith receives its life from Christ himself. Christ is present in faith. And to consider faith apart from Christ is to misunderstand it. Faith points beyond man to God condescending towards us. Neither do we "psychologize" worship when we find its essence in faith, for to believe is to "put on" Christ. Luther's theology of worship rests on God and faith as component parts. The unity of the two is given in Christ, for he is both the revelation of God and the content of faith. As a matter of fact it is Christology which explains the two component parts in worship: Christ is true God and true man in one person. Accordingly, worship also is a unity.

Former Interpretations of Luther's View of Worship

The deficiency of former works on Luther's view of worship is in their basic theological orientation or rather the lack of it. The theologians of the late nineteenth century failed to appreciate the theocentric character of Luther's theology. They proceeded from an alleged antithesis between the "pedagogical" and the "re-presentative" concept of worship.[56] And for all their attempts to harmonize these two views, they could not grasp Luther's liturgics adequately because they had lost contact with the center of his theology. For worship, in order to have its proper place in a total picture of Luther's theology, must be seen against the background of his dualistic-dramatic conspectus of faith and God. Without this perspective, one or the other group of Luther's sayings on worship is sure to become an embarrassment to his interpreters.

The "pedagogical" picture of worship is represented by one of the earliest though now obsolete studies on the liturgics of the reformers. H. Jacoby[57] considers worship "an institute of the mature in faith for the training of the immature." The true agent in Christian worship is the congregation, using the church service as a training ground in faith. There is no room in this definition for God himself, for Jacoby confines himself to Luther's utterances on ceremonies and overlooks God and faith.

Nevertheless, the "pedagogical" view has been widely accepted, although only as one aspect of Luther's liturgics. To this Johannes Gottschick devotes one chapter of his book on Luther's liturgical views and reforms.[58] But instead of refuting it as a

[56] This antithesis is analogous to the distinction between a subjective and and objective picture of the church which nineteenth-century theology bequeathed to this discussion. But this whole approach is foreign to Luther. The "togetherness" of God and faith in his theology forbids any attempt at distinguishing the subjective and objective elements, either in the church or in worship. Cf. Ragnar Bring, "The Subjective and Objective in the Concept of the Church," in A. Nygren (ed.), *This Is the Church* (Philadelphia: Muhlenberg, 1952), pp. 205-225. Of course, some scholars have intimated the deficiencies of the pedagogical and representative views of worship. See Paul Althaus, *Das Wesen des evangelischen Gottesdienstes* (Guetersloh: 1932); G. Mensching, *Die liturgische Bewegung*, p. 25ff; F. Flemming, *Die treibenden Kraefte*.

[57] *Die Liturgik der Reformatoren* (1871-76).

[58] *Luthers Anschauungen vom christlichen Gottesdienst und seine thatsaechliche Reform desselben* (Freiburg: 1887), p. 11ff.

misinterpretation of Luther, he directs his critique against Luther himself and his alleged "pedagogical" interpretation of worship. On the other hand he seeks to "exonerate" Luther by pointing out numerous utterances which counterbalance the "pedagogical" view.[59] In Jacoby's view, the church service has no value for believers. Gottschick takes the opposite stand and tries to define worship as the "believers' common sacrifice of praise."[60] Here too the believing congregation is the agent of worship. The church service is an offering of praise tendered to God. But it becomes meaningless for the "weak" who have no faith which they could "present" to God.

An attempt to resolve this dilemma of "re-presentative" versus "pedagogical" liturgics was made by G. Rietschel. In an article on Luther's teaching on worship, he tries to mediate between the two views by pointing out their mutual connection. While admitting the contrast, he develops certain thoughts which lead from the "re-presentative" idea of worship to the "pedagogical," i.e., to the idea that Christian love makes the congregation of believers responsible for unbelievers in their midst and for the "weak" in faith. But the real merit of Rietschel's study lies not in these attempts at mediating, but in a new approach which points beyond the dilemma. He defines worship as an order, an institution of God, given in the Word and sacraments, and accepted by the receiving congregation in their sacrifice of praise and thanksgiving. Rietschel could have resolved the whole dilemma had he followed this idea to the end. Instead he tried to reconcile two views that are mutually exclusive and utterly foreign to Luther's whole picture of worship.

But the scholars who followed him failed to take up his cue

[59] *Ibid.*, p. 26ff.
[60] *Ibid.*, p. 38f.

and the interpretation of Luther continued along well-worn paths. The "re-presentative" line appears again in Leonhard Fendt's book on the Lutheran service of the sixteenth century.[61] To him Christian worship is an expression of the faith of the church. The Lord's Supper (following the Emmaus story, Luke 24:30ff) is a "meal of joy." The worshipers are the happy "possessors" of faith. Fendt contrasts the dynamic mood of "ownership" in early Christian worship with the static formalism of the medieval mass. The "having" of the early Christians stands out against the *id* of a sacred fetish. This *id* left no room for believers to express their own faith. In Luther, the early Christians' "joy of ownership" broke through again[62] and led to a complete liturgical reorientation and revitalization of the mass. Fendt's interpretation contains important insights. But it suffers from his identification of "faith" with the "mood of ownership," a term inspired more by Schleiermacher than by Luther. As in the "re-presentative" view, worship becomes an end in itself.[63] F. Flemming's study on the driving forces in the Lutheran liturgical renaissance[64] failed to offer a new solution. Indeed, he approaches Luther from the perspective of modern liturgical movements. But Luther cannot be expected to speak his mind when cross-examined by the advocates of contemporary movements and theological factions. Flemming extols "faith" versus "sight." But he fails to understand this contrast eschatologically, as Luther would have done, and arrives at a merely "desensualized" or "uncultic" idea of worship. Man's fellowship with God

[61] *Der lutherische Gottesdienst des 16 Jahrhunderts* (Muenchen: 1923).
[62] *Ibid.*, p. 66, 68.
[63] Fendt does not use the well-known terms *feiernde Gemeinde* (worshiping congregation) and *darstellendes Handeln* (representative action). But his whole theological attitude points in this direction, and the different terminology means little.
[64] *Die treibenden Kraefte.*

is supposed to be independent of "externals." Worship must never be an end in itself. With such statements, Flemming comes back to the "pedagogical" view, in spite of his earnest efforts to present a more balanced approach. The Danish scholar S. Widding[65] arrived at similar results. He too champions a spiritualized picture of worship which leaves little room for an appreciation of the externals of the ordinary church service. And he finds himself unable to resolve the tension between the theme of "ownership" and that of "evangelism."[66] Both he and Flemming are caught in the traffic circle of the "pedagogical" and "re-presentative" view and cannot find the interchange which would lead them on to a new highway carved from the rock foundation of Luther's theology.

This dilemma cannot be resolved unless we understand worship as an institution of God. For in this view, worship becomes a means of salvation and an integral part of the work of God. But apart from it, both the "training school for unbelievers" and the "believers' sacrifice of praise and thanksgiving" are left in mid-air.

The "re-presentative" idea speaks of faith as though it were a static condition which could be isolated from its author—God acting and ever present. The "pedagogical" view founders on the same rock; for it speaks of evangelizing others, as though the Christian congregation could train them without having its own faith renewed. Both views presume to isolate faith from God, as though faith could continue apart from the means of grace. The "pedagogical" view retains the truth that faith is nourished by worship, but forgets that believers need the nourishment as much as unbelievers. The "re-presentative" theory

[65] *Dansk Messe, Tide- og Psalmesang 1528-1573* (Copenhagen: 1955).
[66] *Ibid.*, I, p. 65.

overlooks the fact that the "believers' sacrifice of praise and thanksgiving" depends on their reception of God's grace through the Word and sacraments.

A significant reorientation in the study of Luther's theology of worship was effected by Karl Holl and his school. Here at last we see an attempt to trace Luther's liturgical views back to his basic theological premises. Holl himself sketched this approach in one of his articles.[67] One cannot say that Luther receives full justice in this study.

Holl's well-known misinterpretation of the church also corrupts his understanding of Luther's liturgics. But actually he intended not so much to interpret as to correct Luther. He disapproved of Luther's liturgical conservativism and departed knowingly from the Reformer.[68] The Reformation meant to him a shift of emphasis from the Sacrament to the Word. And the structure of the Lutheran service did not accord with this conviction. He remained within the theological presuppositions of liberal Neo-Protestantism. But his brief article provided the impetus for a more systematic study of Luther's liturgics.

Holl's concept of worship recurs in A. Allwohn's article on worship and justification. Through an exhaustive study of Luther's earlier writings, Allwohn gained new material and insights. By and large he offers no more than a historical review of these writings and an outline of the gradual development of Luther's views on worship. But in the discussion of the material and in the concluding synopsis, he attempts a more comprehensive systematic presentation. His point of departure is the "sole activity" (*Alleinwirksamkeit*) of God. God's "giving and acting" is the basis of worship. Faith as the work of God receives his gifts

[67] *Gesammelte Aufsaetze,* III, p. 220ff.
[68] *Ibid.,* p. 228f.

and is the mark of "worship in the spirit." This theocentric emphasis is the best part of Allwohn's work. Unfortunately he mars it by assuming an antithesis between God and man and by construing a tension between worship as the work of God and the liturgy as the product of sinful men. This antithesis is foreign to Luther who would rather have spoken of an antithesis between theolatry and idolatry. But Allwohn's work remains significant for the attempt, later continued by Theodore Knolle, to interpret Luther's liturgical reforms within the total framework of his theology.

A systematic interpretation of Luther's view of worship should fulfil the following conditions: Against the background of Luther's dramatic dualism, it should present God and faith as the two focal points of his theology. At the same time it should maintain the christological unity of true worship against the background of the incarnation and presence of Christ by faith. This suggests the following scheme for our presentation: The first part deals with worship as the work of God in the church, the second with worship as the work of faith. These two approaches belong together and complement each other. Neither one can be understood correctly apart from the other. For the problem of "theolatry versus idolatry" comes into focus only through the binoculars of "God and faith."

Before unfolding Luther's theology of worship we must delineate the two types of worship which Luther considered mutually exclusive. The antithesis between theolatry and idolatry crystallized in his controversy with Rome about the meaning and proper celebration of the mass.

2

Beneficium and Sacrificium

In the foregoing chapter Luther's theology of worship was developed in relation to the conflict between theolatry and idolatry. We must now turn to the practical application of his theological insights. To this end, we will examine his interpretation of the Lord's Supper as a benefaction (*beneficium*) instituted by Christ, and his rejection of the sacrifice (*sacrificium*) of the mass.[1] There is a real need for a detailed exposition of this subject. Its neglect by other writers accounts for their misinterpretation of Luther's theology of worship.

The History of the Mass: From the Institution by Christ to the Sacrifice of the Mass

"The liturgy now in common use everywhere, like the preaching office, has a high, Christian origin." With these words Luther begins his pamphlet of 1523 on the order of public worship.[2] He is speaking of the Roman mass and finds that in spite of all the accretions and corruptions it derives directly from the Last Supper in the Upper Room. He concedes this to be true in the preface to the *Formula Missae*.[3] The mass has been instituted by

[1] The contrast between *beneficium (testamentum, donum)* and *sacrificium (opus bonum, meritum)* is general wherever Luther refers to worship; cf. *WA* 6, 364; 6, 253; 8, 439; etc.

[2] *WA* 12, 35 (P.E. vol. 6, p. 60).

[3] *WA* 12, 206: "For we cannot deny that the mass and the communion of bread and wine are a rite divinely instituted by Christ himself."

Christ himself.[4] Therefore worship, especially the Lord's Supper, must be seen in relation to Christ. This attitude had two important results: First, Luther sought to reform rather than replace the mass.[5] Second, by the liturgical reforms which he advocated, he meant to bring the mass into closer conformity with its original institution.[6] He was content with the original structure of the mass because he aimed not so much for a change in the external forms of worship[7] as for a radical reappraisal of its meaning and theology. When he pointed to Christ's institution of the Supper, he thought of it not as an example to be copied outwardly, but as a word of God to guide our understanding and faith. He considered the Words of Institution not a law concerning outward ceremonies, but the "gospel in a nutshell," offering forgiveness of sins, life, and salvation.[8] These convictions guided both his criticism and his reform of the mass.

To Luther, the distinctive feature of the Lord's Supper is its simplicity. As Jesus offered bread and wine to his disciples, he used no elaborate ceremonies. These were added later by the

[4] [Following the usage of Luther and the early Reformation, the author uses the term "mass" not only for the communion service of the Roman Catholic church but in a broader sense for any sort of communion service, whether it be conducted by Christ himself, by a Roman priest, or by a Lutheran minister. Trans.]

[5] *WA* 12, 35: "We mean not to abolish, but to restore the church service." 12, 206: "We profess that we never thought nor are thinking of abolishing the worship of God; we mean to purge the one which is commonly in use, but which has been vitiated through some very bad additions, and to indicate how it can be performed in a godly manner."

[6] *WA* 6, 355: "Doubtless our mass will be the better the closer it is to the mass of Christ, and the more precarious, the farther it is from the same." Cf. 6, 523.

[7] Cf. J. Gottschick, *Luthers Anschauungen*, p. 44f; Friedrich Heiler, *Katholischer und evangelischer Gottesdienst*, 2nd ed. (Muenchen: 1925), p. 42.

[8] We note here a significant difference from the Enthusiasts (*Schwärmer*) who demand that Christ's institution should be followed in all its external features. Luther saw in this the danger of a new work righteousness. Cf. L. Fendt, *Der Lutherische Gottesdienst*, p. 104.

church, and not only added, but made obligatory and protected by canon law. For a priest to omit a single word in the Canon was counted a mortal sin, worse than adultery or perjury.[9] And whoever failed to accept or observe these ceremonies was branded a heretic. Thus division and disunity had been caused by all the man-made additions to the Lord's Supper.[10] Luther raised his voice against the particularism of the Roman church, and maintained that all ceremonial laws are conducive to disunity. Jesus had observed such stark simplicity at the institution of the mass, because he meant to abolish ceremonial laws completely and to preserve the unity of his church through the gospel alone.[11] This shows that Luther's criticism of outward ceremonies sprang, not, as has been charged so often, from indifference towards liturgical forms, but from his concern for the Christian conscience, cramped and threatened by ceremonial laws.[12] He did not condemn external ceremonies as such. He only wanted them clearly distinguished from the essential features of Christ's own institution.[13] They had a place in the church here on earth. But Luther objected to the corruption of the mass by which man-made ceremonies sprang up and nearly strangled the Sacrament proper. Where the ceremonial laws tried to supplant the gospel (Christ's original institution), they had "intruded into heaven," where they had no right, and must be ejected.

At the Last Supper, Christ took bread and wine and gave them to the disciples, using external things, and told his disciples to do likewise in remembrance of him. This fact was enough for Luther to prove that the mass must also consist in external actions. He could not agree with the Enthusiasts in their rejection

[9] *WA* 8, 433. [10] *WA* 6, 355. [11] *WA* 6, 354.
[12] Cf. the section below on Faith (Freedom) and Love (Order) in Worship.
[13] *WA* 6, 355.

of all "externals." Ultimately decisive for him was the distinction between externals instituted by God and externals without divine sanction. The latter had been devised by man and could never be granted equal standing with those appointed by Christ himself. Here Luther would not give in. The mass was Christ's own institution and could share this honor with nothing else.

It may seem surprising that Luther included prayers in his list of the parts of the mass which do not properly belong to it. Did he not know that Jesus himself had "given thanks" at the Last Supper? He was well aware of this fact, but he also knew that the prayers of the mass could lay no claim to divine authorship, that many of them, in fact, were contrary to the very meaning of the Eucharist. Nevertheless, he did not condemn them *in toto.* He could see their relative merit. He was not blind to the values of liturgical growth, although his angry criticism of medieval aberrations has gone far to create this impression. He valued highly the chants which the early church had added. He gladly approved of all the parts of the Ordinary, the *Kyrie, Gloria in Excelsis, Credo, Sanctus,* and *Agnus Dei.* These he incorporated in his Latin mass (and also partially in his German mass) and prized them as expressions of the true faith of the church.[14] Through them he remained in the liturgical succession of the early church. He believed that liturgical forms such as these had served to preserve the faith of the common people during the Dark Ages when the mass as a whole had become a piece of idolatry.[15]

But on the whole, Luther found far more that was blame-

[14] *WA* 12, 206. This and other similar utterances prove the faultiness of Rendtorff's theory of a law of liturgical succession. Rendtorff tries to represent Luther as completely indifferent in liturgical matters and claims that it was only the force of circumstances which caused him to employ older liturgical forms.

[15] *WA* 38, 221.

worthy than praiseworthy in the service of the mass in his day. The very core and purpose of the mass, namely the Sacrament according to the institution of Christ, had been half buried by the accretions which were added to it in the course of time. Too many of these liturgical forms stood in rank opposition to the gospel. The profusion of prayers which had overgrown Christ's Words of Institution not only obscured the institution, but were as idolatrous an innovation as King Ahaz' erection of a Syrian altar in the temple (II Kings 16:10ff).[16] Luther's most violent criticism was therefore aimed at the Canon. And in his own orders of service he discarded this part of the mass completely. For contrary to Christ's own Words of Institution, the Canon prayers stamped the mass as a sacrifice rendered to God on behalf of the living and of the dead. Instead of a "eucharist," or an act of thanksgiving for the good gifts of God, the mass had become an act of propitiation by which men sought to appease God. This was incompatible with the gospel, as Luther had come to understand it. The sacrifice of the mass stood against the gospel. Co-existence of the two was out of the question. It could be only the one or the other and Luther chose the gospel.

The theology of sacrifice had brought a whole host of other abominations in its train. People had begun to expect all sorts of benefits and advantages from hearing mass. To Luther, this was the darkest spot in the history of the church, for it had opened the doors wide for trafficking with the mass. Masses were sold and bought and their celebration had become a profitable business for the priesthood. The participation and even the presence of the laity had become unnecessary. The sacrifice of the mass was assumed to influence the material and spiritual well-being of men by remote control.

[16] *WA* 12, 207.

Luther held Pope Gregory the Great responsible for sanctioning the so-called "private" masses which could be celebrated by the priest in the absence of a congregation.[17] To Luther, the Canon and private masses were human inventions and innovations which ought to be fought to the hilt.[18] He knew that his rejection of the Canon touched the very foundations of the Roman church and the papacy. But the thought that the mass, Christ's own institution, had become a trinket to be sold or a charm to be trusted left him no peace.[19] He felt duty bound to give battle for the Word of God and against any human traditions or perversions designed to obscure the very light of the gospel.[20]

This then is the development of the mass from its institution by Christ to its distortion in the medieval doctrine of sacrifice. Luther did not oppose the more elaborate liturgical forms as such. He would have tolerated them gladly had they not corrupted the very meaning and message of the mass. Like any good gardener, Luther was determined to destroy the weeds in order to save the real plants from being hidden and ultimately choked completely.

A similar degeneration of the service is bound to occur whereever liturgical reforms are undertaken with the idea of "enrich-

[17] *WA* 46, 292 (Roerer), TR 2, 244 and 5, 450. Luther refers also to the fact that the Eastern Orthodox church has no private masses. They are an exclusively Roman invention. 39^I, 140, 141.

[18] *WA* Br 5, 594. Cf. 8, 448.

[19] Luther has furnished us with detailed descriptions of the whole medieval corruption of the mass. As early as 1519 he attacked the medieval fraternities who with diverse excesses had made a mockery of the celebration of the mass (*WA* 2, 754ff). In many of his later writings he returned to the same theme, as for example: *WA* 6, 375, 512; 8, 443; 12, 207; 19, 441; 30^II, 293, 305; 50, 204. Cf. Adolph Franz, *Die Messe im deutschen Mittelalter* (Freiburg im Bresgau: 1902), pp. 3-291, for the different superstitions connected with the custom of votive masses and masses for the departed.

[20] *WA* 12, 220.

ing" the service or making it more festive and dignified without reference to the saving acts of Christ which constitute Christian worship. If Luther condemned the Canon prayers which at least had sprung from liturgical soil, how much more critical would he be of the synthetic solemnities concocted in the esthetic and psychological test tubes of modern liturgical reformers.[21] This does not mean that Luther was indifferent toward the liturgy. His concern for the liturgy was determined by his understanding of the gospel.

The Picture of God in the Mass: The God of Mercy, not of Wrath

The difference between their views of God accounts for the divergence between Luther's idea of the mass and that of the Roman church. To Luther, God's character consists in giving, not in receiving. "For this is the true God who gives, but does not take; helps, but asks no help—in short, who does everything and gives everything, yet needs no one. And all this he does freely out of pure mercy and without merit for the unworthy and undeserving, even for the damned and lost. As such he wants to be remembered, confessed, and glorified."[22]

For this reason Luther calls the mass a benefit, not received, but given (*beneficium, non acceptum sed datum*).[23] Far from being able to earn his eternal salvation, man cannot even secure his earthly existence without the grace of God. But the doctrine of the sacrifice of the mass impugns the goodness of the Creator whose

[21] *WA* 6, 355. "In order to celebrate and understand the mass aright we must free ourselves from everything that the eyes or senses may see or find here, whether it be vestments, music, song, fine arts, prayer, wearing or bearing, or whatever else may happen in the mass, until we have grasped and well considered the words of Christ by which he himself performed and instituted the mass and commanded us to perform it." Cf also *WA* 6, 367; 8, 436.

[22] *WA* 30 II, 603.

[23] *WA* 6, 364; cf. 4, 269.

nature is pure beneficence. He demands nothing for himself, but gives gifts to men which they should pass on to their neighbors. For our gifts to God we can demand no credit. They are his. Nor does God ask them of us. He wants nothing but thanks for his gifts, for by giving thanks we confess him as the merciful Giver of every temporal and spiritual gift.[24]

We also acknowledge that they were given to us that we might serve our brother in need. Thus in Luther's idea of God, faith in the Creator, ethics, and worship are closely tied together.[25]

Like creation around us, the mass is God's gift to man, but in no sense is it a gift that man can presume to give to God.[26] What a contrast between God giving his Son for the sins of the world and the pope pretending to offer God his own Son! In the mass of Christ we meet a merciful God reconciling the world to himself, but the mass of Rome reckons with an angry God who must be appeased with sacrifice.

"When they sacrifice, they think it is necessary to placate God. But to wish to appease him is to believe that he is angry and unreconciled, and to believe that he is angry means to expect wrath rather than love, bad instead of good things. Yet if people would receive the Eucharist with profit, they must believe that God has long been reconciled, that out of his consummate love he gives in addition this most perfect gift. Nothing detracts as much from the proper celebration of the Eucharist or is as harmful to the conscience as this sacrilegious opinion of

[24] *WA* 30 II, 602: "By the offering of thanks I receive divine honor. It makes and acknowledges me to be God, even as the offering of works takes his divine honor away, makes him an idol, and does not let him be God." Cf. 10 I, 1, 38.

[25] Cf. Ragnar Bring, *On the Lutheran Concept of the Sacrament* (Stockholm: 1950), pp. 37ff and 51ff.

[26] *WA* 6, 364: "In the mass too we give nothing to Christ; we only receive. . . ." 6, 523: "The mass is a benefaction of the divine promise, offered to men through the hands of the priest." 8, 439: "The Eucharist is not a sacrifice rendered to God, but a gift given to men. . . ." See 8, 444; 6, 364.

the papists that God is angry and needs to be appeased with this sacrifice. If he were not so well reconciled and so full of love, he would never offer or bestow these great riches of his."[27]

Luther's concern for the mass is his concern for a true idea of God. Should he be thought to be angry who reconciled the world to himself in Christ? No angry God would say, "Given and shed for you for the remission of sins." These are the words of a merciful Father who sees the need of his children, grants them his gifts of mercy even when they have forsaken him.[28]

The papists deal with God as though he were a cruel and merciless tyrant, barring the gate of heaven to men.[29] But it is the sin of men and not the anger of God which bars our way to heaven. God in Christ is a God of love who seeks the sinner in mercy.

The Roman mass sees God as a merciless judge. It presumes to prepare an approach to him. But the gospel speaks of heaven opened and Jesus come down to save men in their sins. Rome thinks of God as though he had forsaken man. Luther is only concerned that man should not forsake God. Rome says that man should reach up to God and cause his anger to cease. But the gospel shows God descending in love and defeating the powers which hold man in bondage. With slight exaggeration one might say: Rome sees God in revolt against man. Luther sees man in revolt against God. The sacrifice of the mass presumes to save man from the anger of God. But the mass of Christ freely offers forgiveness for all our sins.[30] As a priest, Luther himself experienced the fear which the Roman concept of sacri-

[27] *WA* 8, 441. Also 8, 442: "And you, foolish and godless papists, do you with your sacrifice invent another God for yourself? Will you never understand that all those who sacrifice are worshipers of idols, and that they commit idolatry as often as they sacrifice?"

[28] *WA* 8, 442; 4, 269.

[29] *WA* 8, 467.

[30] Cf. the whole section in *WA* 8, 466ff.

fice could inspire in the one who was supposed to appease an angry God by his ministrations.[31]

In his lectures on Genesis and in his Table Talks he recalls that during his first mass he had been so terrified by the reading of the Canon that he almost left the altar and discontinued the service. Only by the admonitions of the prior was he enabled to finish the mass.[32] While the exact historical circumstances are open to debate[33] and hard to reconstruct, Luther's recollection of his fear as a novice priest is quite clear from the sources.

The question has often been raised whether this fear was something natural or rather an expression of his religious hypersensitivity.[34] But in the light of what we said above about the picture of God implied in the sacrifice of the mass, and about Luther's polemics against it, the terrors which he experienced at his first mass will seem no more than natural. That the angry God whom we meet in the law inspires fear and terror is a thought which was always characteristic of Luther.[35] It belongs with all the insights which he gained in his cloister cell as he struggled to know a gracious God, and incidentally also with the experi-

[31] *WA* 6, 362: "They have been afraid and made us afraid at the very point where there is no fear and where all our comfort and peace lies." TR 5, 265: "With the words of consecration they scared some of them so much, especially the devout who took the matter seriously, that they trembled over and over when they said the words, 'This is my body etc.'; for these had to be pronounced without hesitation. Here to stammer or to omit a word was counted a grievous sin."

[32] *WA* 43, 382: "When I was yet a monk and for the first time had to read those words in the Canon: *Te igitur, clementissime pater* [for the text of this prayer compare below, p. 61, note 36] and *Offerimus tibi vivo, vero et aeterno,* [We offer unto Thee, the Living, True and Eternal], I was completely stupefied and horrified by these words; for I thought: With what lips do I address such majesty, when even in the sight or in conversation with any prince or king all people must stand in fear?" Cf. *WA* TR 3, 411; TR 2, 133; 4, 384; 5, 86.

[33] Otto Scheel, *Martin Luther* (Tuebingen: 1916-17), II, p. 45ff.

[34] *Ibid.*, II, 34ff, 128f; and Karl Holl, *Gesammelte Aufsaetze,* I, p. 24.

[35] *WA* 40^{I}, 298: "Christ is not Moses, nor a policeman or legislator, but a

ences of everyone who is crushed by the great weight of the law.[36] Correlated with the angry God whom the sacrifice of the mass seeks to appease is the constant dread of sinful man who fears to be found wanting in his restless efforts to satisfy God. The law raises ever higher demands, but it fails to offer that which only the gospel can afford: the assurance of a gracious God.[37] In his later life, when Luther looked back on his monastic life and the first mass he read, he naturally recalled the inward terrors through which he had passed, and his reference to them appears neither unlikely nor unnatural.

Thus the difference between the mass of Christ and the sacrifice of the mass goes back to the difference between a merciful and giving God (Creator and Redeemer) on the one hand and an angry, demanding God on the other. And as this difference cannot be bridged, the two views of God cannot be reconciled either. Luther drew this conclusion in denouncing the picture of an angry God in the mass as a figment of the imagination.[38]

But for a correct understanding of this condemnation, we must remember that while Luther indeed rejected the idea of an angry God, he claimed at the same time that the papists' view of an angry God was really in accordance with their "faith."[39] The

donor of grace, a Saviour and one who has mercy. And to sum it up he is nothing but mere and infinite mercy, given and giving. . . . That doctrine and pestilent opinion of Christ as a lawgiver entered like oil into my bones. . . . Therefore I have a twofold task, first to rid myself of that old ingrained idea of Christ as a lawgiver and judge . . . and second to form a new opinion, that is, true confidence in Christ as the Justifier and Saviour."

[36] Cf. K. Holl, *Gesammelte Aufsaetze*, I, p. 26ff.

[37] *WA* 39^I, 168.

[38] See above, p. 35.

[39] *WA* 8, 442: "When people think and believe that God is angry at someone and needs to be appeased, they do not really think of God, but form an idol in their own heart, for it is clear in the Eucharist that he is not angry nor can he be appeased. But for you he is and remains angry indeed, even as you believe; for you are outside of the faith of the Eucharist and do not believe his promises, differing in no way from a Gentile or a Jew."

wrath of God is the consequence of their misconception of the mass. Instead of thanking the merciful, loving God for his gift in Christ, they despise his goodness, reject the Christ which he offers to them, and presume to offer their own gifts to God. As the prophets of old denounced the sacrifices of Israel, not for their form but for the wrong intent of the worshipers, so Luther decried the Roman mass.

"The purpose of the sacrifices and rites of the law was not that the people through them should be made pleasing to God. From the fall of Adam on, that purpose had been reserved to the sacrifice of Christ alone of which the sacrifices of the law are as a shadow.... It was because of this impiety, which the impious ideas on legal sacrifices confirmed, that the prophets preached so earnestly against sacrifices, not on the matter of form, but with respect to their purpose. For many and frequent sacred rites were conducted at the place appointed by God, and according to his precept. But the purpose was devilish. Likewise we condemn the masses of our adversaries, not because it is wrong simply to celebrate the Lord's Supper (for we also celebrate it, but reverently), but because they add impious ideas of an *opus operatum,* application to the dead and alive, etc."[40] As a result of the sacrifice of the mass, men are crushed by the wrath of God. For to meet God apart from Christ is to meet him in his majesty, and so to confront him is to be crushed.[41] The final judgment of the law here becomes apparent. The differing views of God, in the last analysis, reflect the contrast between a legalistic and an evangelical understanding of the mass.

The Gift of the Mass: Testamentum, not Sacrificium

The God who acts in the mass is merciful and gracious. Luther developed this concept of God from the gift which we

[40] *WA* 40II, 455.

[41] *WA* 40I, 77.

receive in the mass; for in accordance with the institution of Christ, a gift is granted to all who hold the mass. Contrariwise, the mass as a gift offered by men implies a denial of His gift for us. Luther is wont to contrast the two as *testamentum,* God's gift to man, and *sacrificium,* man's gift to God. "There is only one God and only one church. And between the two, the testament mediates from above and the sacrifice from below.[42]

The term "testament" is drawn from the Words of Institution. In his polemical writings of 1520-21 Luther made extensive use of it in order to explain the true meaning of the mass.[43] His preference for the idea of testament has been severely criticised by Yngve Brilioth. Brilioth feels that Luther is guilty of a misinterpretation which prevented him from seeing other equally important moments in the mass, moments which he himself acknowledged in his earlier writings. Allegedly he forced the mass into a legalistic frame of reference through the use of the term "testament," for he therewith introduced a forensic term into the interpretation.[44] A more detailed analysis of the idea of "testament" and Luther's use of it will be the best answer to Brilioth's criticism.

According to Luther, a testament must contain the following elements:[45] There must be, first of all, a testator who prepares for his death and sets up his will, then the testament proper

[42] *WA* 8, 444.

[43] Luther took the picture of the "last will and testament" from Chrysostom where he found it in a homily on Hebrews 9:13ff; cf. his Lectures on Hebrews (*WA* 57, 211f). The most important references in his later writings are *WA* 6, 359; 6, 513f; 8, 444f.

[44] Yngve Brilioth, *Eucharistic Faith and Practice* (London: 1930), p. 101ff. and the introduction, written by him, to *The Babylonian Captivity of the Church* (1928), pp. viii and xvii. It is noteworthy that Joh. Eck also criticized Luther for his forensic understanding of the term "testament."

[45] There are minor variations in the description of the various elements, but no significant difference from the scheme offered in the text.

which contains the will of the testator, the seal by which the testator confirms the validity of his will, the inheritance assigned in the testament, and finally, those to whom the estate is bequeathed. All these elements are found in the mass, instituted by Christ. The testator is Christ who prepares for his death. The testament are his Words of Institution. The seal is the body and blood of Christ. The inheritance is the forgiveness of sins. And the heirs are men of every age and clime.[46]

This comparison depicts impressively the character of the mass as a gift of God. Men can do nothing to qualify for the inheritance. They are recipients and need no merits of their own to claim the bequest.[47] Thus the idea of the testament offered Luther an ideal position for his polemics against the sacrificial understanding of the mass. But actually it had come to him in his exegetical studies, long before the controversies of 1520-21 which prompted him to use it so extensively.

As early as 1516-17 we find an explanation of the term "testament" in Luther's Commentary on Galatians.[48] Commenting on Galatians 3:15, he identifies testament with the promises of God, and contrasts it with the law and righteousness which comes by the law. This lays the stress on the side of the idea of the testament which is also basic to the biblical view of covenant, namely the sovereign act of God who by his promise accepts man into fellowship with himself. It is not an agreement between equals.[49]

[46] Cf. for example Luther's criticism of the idea of sacrifice in the mass (*WA* 8, 444f.) where he shows that it contradicts every element of a testament. "It is impossible for a thing to be a sacrifice and a testament at the same time."

[47] Cf. Brilioth, *op. cit.*, p. 101f: "The strongest side of the testament idea is the central place which it assigns to God's gift."

[48] *WA* 2, 518-21.

[49] See Johannes Behm, "Der neutestamentliche Begriff *diathēke*," in G. Kittel (ed.), *Theologisches Wörterbuch zum Neuen Testament* (Stuttgart: 1935), II, p. 132-137.

The testator and giver of the promise is God. And no man may repeal the covenant and seek to be justified by the law "which was 430 years after." It is this idea of the covenant that gives the term "testament" its depth and dimension.

Further, if God's promises to Abraham could be called a testament (Gal. 3:18), they must imply the incarnation of Christ, for a testament looks forward to the death of the testator. The eternal God had to become man and die in order to fulfil the promise.[50] Thus the two terms Words of Institution (*verba testamenti*) and words of promise (*verba promissionis*) are synonymous.[51] The mass continues and fulfils God's earlier promises.[52] Then as now, God's gifts come through his Word of promise and through our faith.

"Whenever man is to deal with God and receive something from him, it is not up to man to take the initiative and lay the first brick. Rather, without man's seeking or desire God must first come with his promise . . . which he [man] must receive gratefully and confidently trust the divine promise."[53] This makes the Words of Institution the most important part of the mass. And their neglect explain its corruption;[54] for by their very wording they preclude the theology of sacrifice and are in themselves the best summary of the gospel.

This identification of the Words of Institution with the earlier promises of God shows also that Luther's view of the mass was not, as has been charged, vitiated by the juridical term "testament." For back of it stood the covenant idea of the Old Testa-

[50] *WA* 2, 521. Cf. 6, 514, and 8, 444.

[51] This idea is prominent in *Sermon von dem Neuen Testament* and *De abroganda missa privata;* cf. *WA* 6, 356ff and 8, 436.

[52] *WA* 6, 357.

[53] *WA* 6, 356.

[54] *WA* 11, 432; 6, 362.

ment. The only significant difference between the idea of "promise" and that of "testament" lies in the reference to the death of Christ which the latter implies.

We may add here another aspect which shows the value of the idea of testament. In accordance with Hebrews 9:16 where the author sees the testament validated by the death of Christ, Luther finds a natural and necessary connection between the testament and the body and blood of Christ, offered up in death.[55] This is his reason for the intimate bond between testament and sacrament (that is, the elements: bread and wine). It is important to note that the idea of sacrament is not in addition to, but an integral part of the testament. The difference between the testament proper (the promise, the Words of Institution) and the Sacrament (bread and wine) lies *within* the picture of testament and both ideas are valid only in their relationship to each other. Luther is often thought to have considered the Sacrament a mere "confirmation" or "pledge" and the elements a sort of accidental appendage. This is a misunderstanding. Luther found a contrast, not between testament and sacrament, but between the idea of testament (including the sacrament) and that of sacrifice. When he accused the Roman theologians of overemphasizing the sacramental aspect, he decried not the Sacrament as such but its perversion into an offering rendered to God.[56]

Luther's idea of testament has also been objected to on the grounds that it tends to ignore the aspect of communion, allowing the worshiper to remain purely passive.[57] But this objection loses its validity when we recall the dominant features in Luther's idea of testament. Here the heirs have their assured place. A

[55] *WA* 6, 359.
[56] See for example, *WA* 6, 363 and 6, 518, etc. See also R. Bring, *On the Lutheran Concept*, p. 39f.
[57] See Y. Brilioth, *op. cit.*, p. 102.

testament without heirs is unthinkable. It is equally unthinkable for Luther that the heirs should only admire the inheritance without taking possession of it.[58] They must receive it in faith and profit by it.[59] Their unworthiness cannot prevent them from accepting the gift, but will find expression in their willingness to receive it thankfully, and to praise the testator.[60] To watch the mass without receiving it would contradict the deepest meaning of the idea of testament. Of course it is true that, according to this idea, the inheritance is a reality whether it is accepted or not. But this fact does not stem from a juridical approach on the part of Luther, as has been charged. It derives from the character of God's activity, for the inheritance has real existence whether or not man believes in it. As a matter of fact, it is so real that it does not allow for any neutrality on the part of man; the non-acceptance of the gift cannot place him outside of the sphere of God's activity, for it expresses a definite attitude of faith. Thus even the attitude of the spectator who refuses to accept the gift betrays faith in the attempt to gain merit before God through his piety, his religious spectatorship. This attitude reveals an understanding of the mass as sacrifice rather than testament.[61]

The tendency to substitute a passive admiration of the host for its active reception lies at the bottom of the sacrifice of the

[58] This misunderstanding is found in F. Graebke's study, *Die Konstruktion der Abendmahlslehre Luthers*, (Leipzig: 1908), p. 37, 49f. Graebke finds the moment of communion left out in Luther's doctrine of the Lord's Supper. But it is open to dispute whether or not this criticism is sufficiently justified by Luther's early references to a "Communion without eating and drinking." For Luther considered this possibility an emergency measure, necessitated by the fact that the Roman church had robbed the people of the Sacrament. These remarks have moreover no reference to the testament idea, for this idea gives expression to the fact that the mere spectator of the mass (that is, of the inheritance) is holding the bequest in contempt.

[59] *WA* 8, 445.

[60] *WA* 6, 519.

[61] R. Bring, *On the Lutheran Concept*, p. 47ff.

mass. It is the attitude of the beggar who, instead of accepting the alms which a benevolent ruler grants him, wants to use them to secure his ruler's favor. The aspect of receiving constitutes a necessary part of the mass as testament. "Who has ever heard that a man performs a good work by receiving an inheritance? He receives a benefit. Likewise in the mass we give nothing to Christ but receive from him—unless standing still and accepting benefits may be referred to as a good work.[62]

In conclusion, we must review briefly Luther's stand with regard to the elevation, for again it reflects the contrast between testament and sacrifice.

The elevation formed the climax of the medieval mass and was intended to demonstrate the "gift of the mass."[63] When the priest had changed the elements into the body and blood of Christ he displayed them for the people to worship. This act had attracted to itself all kinds of superstitious beliefs and practices.[64] And these very abuses explain Luther's violent criticism of the elevation.[65] Nevertheless he did not reject it completely.[66] He was willing to tolerate it. The seeming ambiguity is explained from his theological principles. He accepted or rejected liturgical forms according to their theological meaning. As an expression

[62] *WA* 6, 364. Cf. 8, 437.

[63] For the origin and meaning of the elevation cf. P. Browe, *Die Verehrung der Eucharistie im Mittelalter* (Muenchen: 1933), and T. W. Drury, *Elevation in the Eucharist, its History and Rationale* (Cambridge: 1907).

[64] See P. Browe, *op. cit.*, p. 50f; A. Franz, *op. cit.*, pp. 32f, 101ff; and J. A. Jungmann, *Missarum Sollemnia* (Wien: 1949), II, p. 250ff.

[65] *WA* TR 5, 265. Cf. TR 5, 621: "That superstitious idolatry, . . . without any testimony of the fathers and tradition, has been invented only in order to confirm errors such as the adoration [of the elements] and transsubstantiation, and [it] obscures the proper observation of the Sacrament."

[66] For example, in the *Deutsche Messe*, *WA* 19, 11: "We do not want to abolish the elevation but retain it because it goes well with the German Sanctus and signifies that Christ has commanded us to remember him" (P.E. VI, p. 183). Cf. *WA* TR 5, 308.

of the idea of testament, he was willing to tolerate the elevation. The priest might hold up the elements (even though no such rite had been appointed by Christ) in order to show the people the pledge of God's covenant. "When he elevates the host, he addresses not God but us, as though to say to us: 'See, this is the seal and sign of the testament wherein Christ has bequeathed to us remission of sins and eternal life.' This agrees with the song of the choir: 'Blessed is he that cometh in the name of the Lord.' Hereby we testify that in the mass we receive benefits from God, not offer or give anything to him."[67]

But Luther was bitterly opposed to the elevation if it was meant as a display of our gifts to God. And he could not overcome the suspicion that this was the motive that had prompted the introduction of the elevation.[68]

Luther has often been criticized for rejecting the sacrificial element in the mass as completely as he did. Did he not neglect an essential line of New Testament thought? Is the gospel complete without the idea of sacrifice? We shall leave this question till later.[69] Suffice it to say that Luther had no intention of striking the idea of sacrifice from the gospel. On the contrary, he objected to the medieval theology of the mass for the very reason that it corrupted the proper biblical meaning of sacrifice. The papists had made a sacrifice of that which is no sacrifice and at the same time neglected to bring those sacrifices which are pleasing to God.[70] Luther did not reject the idea of sacrifice at all.

[67] *WA* 6, 359. Cf. 7, 694; 6, 366; and 8, 447.

[68] *WA* 8, 447.

[69] See the chapter on The Priestly Sacrifice of the Believers.

[70] *WA* 8, 421: "A pious and faithful conscience must rightfully fear the error of calling or holding that to be a sacrifice, which God and the Scriptures most certainly do not call a sacrifice. And it will accept as sacrifice only that which God constantly calls a sacrifice. For what temerity could be more insane than that which makes its own mouth the voice of heaven and calls that a

Rather, he gave it its rightful place in the faith and life of the church.[71]

The Use[72] of the Mass: Faith, not Works

"Faith" and "works" are the labels which indicate differing modes of appropriating (*gebrauchen*) the mass. God's merciful gift demands faith alone and precludes every attempt on the part of man to demand credit for his works.[73] God's promises become null and void unless man submits passively to the works of God; for his mercy can be used only by faith. And it would be vain presumption for man to make himself the giver where he is only the recipient.[74] But the Roman mass had become a "work" of men.[75] Luther's struggle against the abuse of the mass sprang therefore from the very core of the gospel of the Reformation: righteousness is by faith, and not by works.

The terms which he used to clarify this antithesis in respect to the mass are *opus operatum* and *opus operantis*. Medieval scholasticism had introduced these expressions in order to dis-

sacrifice and worship of God which God himself does not call a sacrifice or worship of God? For what else is this but making gods according to our own reason and judging things divine by our own understanding?" 6, 368: "It is all upside down: That which belongs to the mass, we attribute to ourselves and want to do it by ourselves. And that which we ought to do, we attribute to the mass, . . . all this comes from unlearned, false preachers."

[71] *WA* 6, 522, 367.

[72] [The German word *gebrauchen*, translated as "use" in connection with the mass, can be explained only by using English words from "celebration" to "reception" and "appropriation." All of them together express what the German word implies. Ed.]

[73] *WA* 8, 436: "The promise requires the faith of those who accept it and its pledge." 10 II, 212: "The use of the mass cannot consist in offering and working, but solely in receiving and in mere passivity."

[74] *WA* 8, 443: "Men's part in the Eucharist is not to sacrifice or give, but to believe and accept."

[75] *WA* 6, 512: "The third captivity of the same sacrament is that most impious abuse by which it is firmly held in the church today that the mass is a good work and a sacrifice."

tinguish the sacraments in the Old from those in the New Testament.[76] The former were supposed to avail only if there was faith (*ex opere operantis*), while the mass, as an example of the latter, was supposed to take effect through the mere performance of the act (*ex opere operato*). As a "work of merit," the mass was expected to earn the grace of God. Luther rejected this distinction between the sacraments of the Old and New Testament and maintained that the latter also required faith on the part of the recipient. He saw no benefit in the mass unless it is performed with the personal participation of the one who uses the mass (*opus operantis*).

Of course, it is important to realize that Luther vested the borrowed scholastic terms with new meaning. From the standpoint of scholasticism, the term *opus operantis* signified man's disposition for the reception of grace. And as seen from this angle, faith might appear as a human prerequisite for validating the grace of God. This would lead to a misinterpretation of Luther. It is well known that he stressed the validity of the sacrament irrespective of the faith of the recipient.

The Sacrament, like all the gifts of the Creator, is a good gift of God. Neither the character nor the validity of the work of God is at stake. Where the mass is held, there God is always at work and scatters his gifts prior to and independent of the disposition of man. But Luther was concerned with the *use* of the mass. God's gifts must be used with gratitude. And man cannot prove his thankfulness for them except by faith. The word of promise, the core and center of the mass, requires faith.

"There are many who believe the mass or sacrament to be, as they say, *opus gratum opere operati,* that is, a work that is pleasing to God in itself, although the ones who perform it are

[76] Reinhold Seeberg, *Lehrbuch der Dogmengeschichte* (1913), III, p. 461f.

not pleasing to him. From this they conclude that there is value in holding many masses, though they be used unworthily. I do not care what others think, but such myths do not please me. For there is no created thing or work that would not in itself please God, as it is written in Genesis 1 that God saw all his works and was pleased with them. But what happens if we abuse bread, wine, gold, and every good thing, although they in themselves please God? Condemnation comes of it.

"Likewise here, the nobler the sacrament is, the greater the harm that comes to the whole church from its abuse, for it has been instituted, not for its own sake that it might please God, but for our sake that we might use it aright, exercise our faith with it, and become pleasing to God through it. It is of no benefit as long as it is only *opus operatum*. It must become *opus operantis*. As bread and wine do nothing but harm if they are not used aright, however much they may please God, so it is not enough for the sacrament to be performed [i.e. *opus operatum*]. It must be appropriated in faith [i.e. *opus operantis*]."[77]

The abuse of the mass lay in the claim that it imparted grace irrespective of the personal faith of the recipient. "Where faith is dead and the word of faith is silenced, works and traditions about works soon take their place. . . . So has it been with the mass which by the teaching of godless men has been changed into a good work which they themselves call a *opus operatum* by which they presume to be able to do all sorts of things before God. . . . They have lied in saying that the mass is valid because it is an *opus operatum*."[78]

The mass had become a good work by which a man might earn the favor of God without being inwardly affected and renewed. Scholasticism held that the mass was a God-pleasing

[77] *WA* 2, 751.

[78] *WA* 6, 520.

work, even though it might not be used in faith. It was this perversion of a good work of God's that had made it a bane rather than a blessing to man.[79]

The more basic reason for this interpretation of the mass lay in the separation of grace and faith. To Luther, God's grace and its appropriation by faith belong together, for God's acts concern man as a person. Grace is not a quality within God but is God himself dealing with man here and now. Wherever men receive the Sacrament without faith, they experience not its "proper work" but its "strange work"—God's judgment and wrath toward all those who abuse the gifts of his mercy.[80]

Thus Luther's criticism of the *opus operatum* idea was basically directed against a mistaken objectivation (*Verselbstaendigung*) of the mass. Grace and faith had been separated from each other unnaturally. This objectivation made the mass a good work and an obstacle to faith.[81] The works of God benefit us as long as they are used in faith, for it is only by faith that God's work as a gift of grace enters man as a person. To believe is to possess (*"Glaubst du, so hast du"*). Grace is not a supernatural, impersonal force, but a fellowship between God and man by which God enters the life of man and turns his unbelief into faith. It is the living Christ coming to man through Word and sacrament.

But the mass as *opus operatum* belied the very meaning of faith. Everyone must believe for himself. One cannot believe by proxy. What does it avail to read mass after mass?[82] None but the believers receive the fruit of the mass anyhow.[83] Nor is it

[79] *WA* 2, 751.

[80] *WA* 6, 526.

[81] *WA* 6, 517, 518.

[82] *WA* 6, 521: "Each one can make the mass useful only for himself, by his own faith; he can communicate it to no one else." 8, 443: "It obviously follows that the Eucharist or mass cannot be applied or communicated to anyone else."

[83] *WA* 6, 365.

possible to distinguish between different kinds of masses and to expect varied material or spiritual benefits from them. The only valid distinction is whether men come to faith or not.[84] For God is always ready to act and to grant his love to the believer, but he is also ready to condemn the man who vaunts his own "good works" instead of believing God's gracious promises.[85] More important than liturgical correctness is the believing acceptance of the mass. The former springs from man's attempt to clear himself before God, the latter from his trust in the clearance which God has wrought for him in Christ. After all, justification comes by neither moral nor ceremonial works, but is freely given to those who believe in Christ.[86] So the righteousness of faith forms the only proper approach to the mass. Here too one must choose between benefaction and sacrifice.

Must we renounce the term "sacrifice" completely? Not necessarily. But the sacrifices of the New Testament are spiritual sacrifices requiring spiritual persons.[87] A man must be good before he can do good works and render spiritual sacrifices to God. "We do not become just by doing just works, but having been made just, we do just works."[88] A justified man will express his gratitude by rendering sacrifice, and his sacrifice will be acceptable to God because of the faith of the man. "There are works which are good, but not before God who considers first the personal goodness of a man and then his works. Compare Genesis 4 [:41] where God regarded first Abel and then his sacrifice but

[84] *WA* 6, 375: "One mass is as another; there is no difference, except in the faith. For he who believes the most receives the greatest benefit. The mass serves for faith and for nothing else."

[85] *WA* 6, 526.

[86] *WA* 40 II, 454; 6, 364.

[87] *WA* 12, 186: "There are only spiritual sacrifices in the church, as St. Peter says [I Pet. 2:5], i.e. sacrifices in spirit and in truth. These can be offered by no one except a spiritual person, a Christian who has the Spirit of Christ."

[88] *WA* 1, 226.

did not regard Cain or his sacrifice, although outwardly his offering was as good as Abel's."[89] But the same offering becomes an abomination if the giver thereby seeks to purchase his own salvation from God. It is only in faith that we can speak of the sacrifice of the justified.[90]

The Order of the Mass: Missa Communionis, not Missa Privata

A kind donor gives his gifts to be accepted. God gives his gifts to be received by men. The mass as a gift of God calls for a congregation to receive the gift. The importance of faith on the "receiving end" implies the presence of a worshiping congregation. Luther required this for all the means of grace. As the proclamation of the Word demands a listening audience, so neither baptism nor the mass are possible without recipients.[91] The sacraments were instituted, not for a solitary individual, but for the whole church in communion.[92] The Roman practice of "private masses" therefore contradicts the original institution of the Sacrament.[93] Christ at the Last Supper did not keep the Sacrament for himself; he gave it to the disciples.[94] This is why his gift of atonement could benefit the "many" for whom he would suffer and die.

As Jesus spoke the Words of Institution to be heard by all the disciples, so he offered bread and wine to be eaten and drunk

[89] *WA* 10 I, 1, 120.

[90] Cf. the chapter on The Priestly Sacrifice of Believers.

[91] *WA* 12, 215: "As it is absolutely absurd so to pervert the ministry of the Word that one would preach the Word publicly where there is no audience and preach to himself in an empty building or under the sky, so is it the greatest perversion to have the ministers prepare and adorn the table of the Lord where there are no guests who could eat and drink, so that they, who should minister to others, eat and drink alone at an empty table and in a deserted building." Cf. 38, 193.

[92] *WA* 38, 191.

[93] *WA* 39 I, 154.

[94] *WA* 8, 438; 8, 439.

by all. Both his words and acts established the Supper as a meal of fellowship. Therefore for the celebration of the mass it is essential that the work of Christ be proclaimed, as it is done most succinctly in the Words of Institution, and that bread and wine be distributed to the congregation. Actually the Words of Institution are the center of the mass.[95] They must never be obscured. But the congregation must hear them and learn their message. For this reason Luther criticised the inferior position in the Canon of the Words of Institution, and the rubric which provided that they be read inaudibly.[96] He called for a service in the vernacular that these all-important words might be understood by all the people.[97] In the medieval church, the congregation had been kept totally ignorant of them; for even the German expositions of the mass omitted the Canon and therewith the Words of Institution.[98] The main purpose of the German liturgies, published in the wake of the Reformation, was to remedy this omission and to restore the Words of Institution to the people.[99] For the same reason Luther called for the distribution of both bread and wine to the congregation. "To consider communion in both forms a heresy is an insult to Christ and to the gospel, and to the Sacrament itself, for Christ instituted it under both forms, and the church has used it thus for many centuries, as no one can deny."[100] To receive bread and wine is not a privilege of the clergy only but is the right of every Christian which cannot be

[95] *WA* 6, 255.
[96] *WA* 6, 362 and 8, 433.
[97] *WA* 6, 362; 6, 524; 7, 694.
[98] Cf. A. Franz, *op. cit.*, pp. 630ff. and 677ff.
[99] L. Fendt, *op. cit.*, p. 94. Concerning the first German masses see Julius Smend, *Die evangelischen deutschen Messen bis zu Luthers deutscher Messe* (Goettingen: 1896), as well as Fendt, *op. cit.*, p. 82ff, and Brilioth, *op. cit.*, p. 110f.
[100] *WA* 6, 79.

taken from him.[1] Only the false teachings of transsubstantiation and of the sacrifice of the mass had caused the cup to be denied to the laity.

At first Luther was content with establishing these principles and took no practical steps toward their realization. He expected a council of the church to deal with the problem and to proclaim communion in both forms.[2] In the meantime he was willing to abide by the present status so long as the congregation's right was granted in principle. But when the Roman church would not so much as grant the justice of Luther's claim, he refused to compromise any longer and insisted on the cup for the laity.[3] He was convinced that the mass could never have become a sacrifice if the distribution to the people had been retained.[4] For the practice of holding private masses had developed with the interpretation of the mass as a sacrifice. As such, the mass had become an affair between the priest and God, so the distribution could be omitted. Even with no congregation present all sorts of benefits were expected of the mass, for the Roman church considered a mass valid even though the officiant should be the only communicant. But Luther could not reconcile the self-communion of the priest with Christ's own institution[5] and suspected that it had replaced the distribution to the people.

[1] *WA* 6, 501.

[2] For example, he discusses it in the Communion Sermon of 1519 (*WA* 2, 742-58), later in Explanation of Some Articles, 1520 (*WA* 6, 78-83); Answer to the Pamphlets, 1520 (*WA* 6, 137-41); and *Ad schedulam inhibitionis*, 1520 (*WA* 6, 144-53). Even in the Sermon on the New Testament, of 1520, this question remains in the background, although Luther treats it critically (*WA* 6, 374).

[3] When Luther resigned himself to the fact that a council was impossible (*De captivitate*, *WA* 6, 406f), he had begun to doubt the competence of a council in deciding such a question. In the same work he called the retention of the cup the first captivity of the Sacrament.

[4] *WA* 8, 439.

[5] *WA* 18, 32.

At times it may appear as though Luther had absolutely rejected any kind of self-communion. But one ought to note the connection of his words. He condemned self-communion because he scorned the belief that the mere performance of a private mass could yield imaginary benefits for the living and dead and all sorts of other causes.[6] But he permitted self-communion if the elements were received not only by the priest, but also by the congregation.

The Sacrifice of Christ and the Sacrifice of the Mass

In the preceding paragraphs we have studied the antithesis of "benefaction" versus "sacrifice" from different angles. We also intimated that basically it is a contrast between two ways of salvation, the way of the gospel and that of the law. But we could not examine the hub before taking the spokes apart. Now we shall concentrate on the central problem of the mass, its relation to the atoning work of Christ. While Luther rejected the interpretation of the mass as a sacrifice, he accepted and used that term for Christ's atoning work.[7]

It is hardly surprising that Luther spoke of Christ's work as a sacrifice. He simply followed the New Testament and theological tradition. It is true that he described the atonement more often as a struggle between Christ and the forces of darkness.[8] But he also used the figures of sacrifice as an instance of the love of God in Christ for us. Commenting on Galatians 2:20 he says:

"Christ is the Son of God who out of pure love gave himself to redeem me. In these words Paul depicts beautifully the priesthood and offices of Christ. The latter consist in placating God,

[6] Compare *WA* 6, 525 in *De captivitate.* Against self-communion see 8, 438f; 39 I, 156 and 50, 203.

[7] *WA* 12, 175; 15, 766; 18, 23.

[8] R. Bring, *Dualismen hos Luther,* p. 103ff and G. Aulén, *Christus Victor* (London: 1950), p. 119ff.

interceding, and praying in behalf of sinners, offering himself as the victim for their sins, redeeming them, etc. . . . With Paul one might define Christ as the Son of God who without any merit or righteousness on our part, out of pure love and mercy, gave and offered himself to God as a sacrifice for us miserable sinners that he might sanctify us forever."[9] This quotation makes Christ's sacrifices a part of his humiliation by which he took the sins of the world on himself and bore condemnation and death, the rightful destiny of men. That he who knew no sin was made sin for us is his sacrifice. He the innocent submitted to the law that he might free us who are the guilty. His sacrifice is included in the merciful plans of God who sees mankind in bondage and gives himself in order to free us.[10]

This idea of sacrifice has nothing in common with the theology of sacrifice which underlies the medieval understanding of the mass. According to the scholastics it is Christ as a man *(qua homo)* who stands before God on behalf of men. He points up the merits which gain recognition for those who share in them through masses and indulgences. The sacrifice is not, as for Luther, an act of God's mercy, but a human attempt to satisfy God.[11] And we can understand Luther's contention that Christ is sacrificed and crucified again in the mass. "But I fear, no, alas, I see that your sacrificing amounts to offering up Christ anew, as Hebrews 6:6 predicted: They crucify to themselves the Son of God afresh, and put him openly to shame."[12] "Christ was once offered to bear the sins of many, yet they go ahead and sacrifice him daily more than a hundred thousand times in the world, wherewith they deny in

[9] *WA* 40 I, 297, 298.
[10] *WA* 40 I, 298.
[11] *WA* 8, 466-467. Here Luther describes the scholastic idea of Christ as the one who satisfies the demand of an unjust God (*satisfactor exactionis iniqui dei*).
[12] *WA* 8, 421. Cf. 15, 770.

their hearts and by their deeds that Christ put sin to nought and that he died and rose again."[13]

A blasphemy such as this precluded any possibility of linking the sacrifice of the mass with the sacrifice on Calvary. "I would rather be burned at the stake than admit that in celebrating mass a priest with his work, be it good or evil, is equal or higher than my Lord and Saviour Jesus Christ. Thus we must be and remain divided and against each other forever."[14]

Protestant theology is wont to contrast the continual repetition of the sacrifice in the mass with the uniqueness *(Einmaligkeit)* of the death of Christ. The difference between the two is conceived in numerical terms, according to whether the sacrifice is repeated or not.[15] But is this really the salient point of Luther's critique? One could of course point to the well-known passages in Hebrews 7:27, 10:11ff, etc., and to Luther's charge that Christ's crucifixion is being repeated in the mass.

But this argumentation could easily be countered by the more recent Catholic expositions on the mass. Modern Roman Catholic theologians seek to prove that Luther's objections miss the point. What Luther rejected, they say, was but a caricature of the "catholic" understanding of the mass. Admittedly his own contemporaries, under the influence of Nominalism, had lost the proper meaning of the mass. But Luther himself was not free from the spirit of Nominalism. So the whole Reformation controversy boils down to a skirmish between two factions of a theological school which has been disposed of long ago.

So much for the modern Catholic view. Of course the alleged

[13] *WA* 18, 29. [14] *WA* 50, 204. Cf. 6, 367.

[15] This idea is fairly common. It is also the view of a group of outstanding theologians who in a report to the Conference on Faith and Order in Lund interpreted the Reformation criticism in this way. See *Ways of Worship* (London: 1951), p. 33.

Nominalism of Luther is open to serious doubt. But it must be admitted that Thomas Aquinas and his modern interpreters make no use of the idea of a repetition of Christ's sacrifice. In fact, they reject it categorically.[16] They introduce such terms as *repraesentatio* (representation) and *memoria passionis Christi* (remembrance of Christ's passion) and seem to take the wind right out of the sails of their Protestant opponents and perhaps even of Luther.[17] Was Luther fighting against windmills in his repudiation of a mass theory that was not even sanctioned by the best medieval authorities? Might not the terms *repraesentatio* and *memoria* point up a solution of the age-old controversy between Romanists and Protestants?

This is not the place to discuss the ecumenical possibilities and prospects of our day. But it might help in undergirding these discussions to show that the question of "repetition" is not the salient point of Luther's critique of the mass.[18]

It is not only with reference to the mass that Luther rejected the principle of repetition. He detected the same tendency in every form of work righteousness, for work righteousness, instead of accepting the work of God for us, seeks to amass and accumu-

[16] Gabriel Biel, whose commentary on the mass Luther studied, rejects the thought of a repetition of the sacrifice of Christ (*WA* TR 3, 192, 564). Cf. Herman Degering, *Luthers Randbemerkungen zu Gabriel Biels Collectiorium* (Weimar: 1933). For the treatment of the problem by scholasticism cf. F. S. Renz, *op. cit.*, I, pp. 725-816; and D. Stone, *op. cit.*, I, pp. 314-344.

[17] Iserloh proceeds from the assumption that in the Reformation controversies the Catholic standpoint did not receive its due for want of an able advocate. Compare his book, *Der Kampf um die Messe* (Muenster in Westfalen: 1952), especially pp. 8, 56ff.

[18] The above-mentioned Commission on Faith and Order would welcome an ecumenical exchange concerning these questions. Such a discussion would have to be conducted not only with the Roman Catholics, but also with present-day Anglicans where the same thoughts have found a home. A simple solution for the question of sacrifice cannot be expected as long as one seems to believe that the concept of *repraesentatio* is able to remove all misunderstandings (*Ways of Worship*, p. 33, 204ff).

late ever more "good works" in order to appease God.[19] So it amounts to crucifying Christ anew, for it acts as if the sacrifice on Calvary had never been made. "All works which are done to atone for sin or to escape [eternal] death are nothing but blasphemy, a denial of God, and an insult to the sacrifice which Christ has made and to his blood, for they presume to do what Christ's blood alone must do."[20] The sacrifice of the mass is only one more instance, among many, of the attempt to influence God by offerings of "good works," or, as Luther wrote in his Large Commentary on Galatians:

"St. Paul contends hotly against the Antichrist because the latter abolishes grace and denies the gracious work of Christ our high priest, who gave himself a sacrifice for our sins. So to deny Christ means no less than to spit and trample on him, to usurp his place, and to say: 'I shall justify and save you.' 'What with?' 'With masses, pilgrimages, indulgences, observance of the monastic rule, and the like.' "[21]

So the mass is rank idolatry in the eyes of Luther. It smacks of legalism. It presumes to give to God what man can only receive.[22] And for the same reason that people had tried to accumulate other "good works," they had celebrated the sacrifice of the mass in feverish repetition. What Luther condemned was not so much the number of worship services, as the tendency behind them and the total disregard of the work of Christ which they implied. Doubtless he would have rejected the legalism of the mass quite as violently under the name *repraesentatio* or *memoria;* for to him the difference between the sacrifice on Calvary and that of the mass was more than one of number.[23]

[19] *WA* 30 II, 610.
[20] *WA* 18, 24. Cf. 40 I, 328; 8, 421.
[21] *WA* 40 I, 300.
[22] *WA* 40 I, 602, 604.
[23] We agree with F. W. Schmidt when he says (*op. cit.,* p. 25): "While the theological vocabulary may have changed, we must maintain that the Re-

Returning to our original question, we ask again: How are the sacrifice on Calvary and the mass mutually related? Granted that the mass is not a repetition of that greater and earlier sacrifice, what is the relation between the atonement wrought on the cross and the remission of sins offered in every mass? To answer this question, Luther distinguishes the *acquisition* of the remission of sins on Calvary from its *distribution* in the means of grace.[24] Once and for all the remission of sins has been procured, but it is offered and distributed again and again. Christ's work had been promised from the dawn of history, and it has benefited mankind in every time and clime.[25] We are forgiven daily, as again and again we receive the gift of God's love. And it is precisely this gracious offer of forgiveness which forbids the sacrificial understanding of the mass. Far from being another sacrifice of Christ, the mass should encourage us to trust in the one and only sacrifice of Calvary.[26] It makes little difference if the mass should be called a *repraesentatio* of the passion of Christ; even so it remains a work of man rather than the distribution of the work of Christ.

Luther found the connecting link between the mass and the atoning work of Christ in the words: "this do in remembrance of me." Medieval theologians had understood these words to read: "do a representation of my sacrifice."[27] But Luther interpreted

formers rejected not only a clumsy popular theology, but that they fathomed the problem to its very depths." Cf. Gerhard Kappner, *Sakrament und Musik,* (Guetersloh: 1952), p. 44f.

[24] *WA* 18, 203.

[25] *WA* 18, 203: "The acquisition happened once at the cross. But the distribution has happened often, before and after, from the beginning of the world to its end; for seeing that he resolved to procure it once and for all, it did not matter whether he distributed it through his Word before or after, as can easily be proved from the Scriptures."

[26] It is well known that in his later years, Luther was troubled in conscience by the fact that as a Roman priest he had "butchered" Christ. *WA* TR 2, 417.

[27] Compare Iserloh's criticism of Luther, *op. cit.,* p. 149.

them in accordance with Paul's words: "you proclaim the Lord's death until he comes" (I Cor. 11:26).[28] Here the remembrance was a message, there a sacrifice.

We shall deal with the connection of "proclamation" and "remembrance" later on. Here we note only a certain ambiguity in Luther's early lectures on Hebrews. He was still using the term "sacrifice" for the *memoria oblationis Christi* (remembrance of Christ's sacrifice), but interpreted it partly as a spiritual sacrifice—a mortification of the flesh—and partly as a proclamation.[29] Later on, he rejected the identification of "remembrance" and "sacrifice" emphatically, for, says he, if the remembrance of Christ's death should represent a repetition of it, the same would hold true of the remembrance of his birth and resurrection.[30] The idea of sacrifice which he rejected, however, was always that of an atoning sacrifice.[31] He could well conceive of the remembrance as a thank offering for the work of Christ. But never can it be a human work, neither in the form of a "liturgical representation" nor as mystical devotion.[32] It is the work of God himself who offers bread and wine for the forgiveness of sins.

The practical consequence of Luther's rejection of the sacrificial theology of the mass was his emphatic repudiation of the *Canon Missae.* He removed it entirely because it was a concentrated liturgical expression of the theology of sacrifice. In a sermon of 1526,[33] and in his work *Vom Greuel der Stillmesse* (On the Abomination of the Canon) of 1525,[34] he examined the prayers of the Canon individually and proved their incompatibility with the sacrifice of Christ. The following moments in the Canon were most objectionable to him.

[28] *WA* 1, 334; 6, 373. [29] *WA* 57, 213 and 217 (Hb).
[30] *WA* 8, 421. [31] *WA* 30 II, 610. [32] *WA* 30 II, 611.
[33] *WA* 15, 764-74. [34] *WA* 18, 22-36.

First of all, he pointed out that the prayers of the Canon offer ordinary bread and wine as propitiation to God.[35] The prayers *Te igitur* and *Hanc igitur oblationem* especially speak of these earthly gifts as the sacrifices with which the priest enters into the presence of God.[36] Bread and wine take the place of the sacrifice of Christ, for the reference is to the unconsecrated elements, as the prayer *Quam oblationem* proves.[37] As a matter of fact, Luther noted a lack of order and logic in the whole prayer act preceding the Words of Institution.[38] Of course, it is absurd to expect the same spiritual benefits from the earthly elements as from Christ's death on Calvary. Luther's faith in the Creator would not allow the gifts of this earth to become a means of earning the grace of God. We have the gifts of creation, not to gain the grace of God, but to serve our fellow-men. And to quote the sacrifices of Abel, Melchizedek, and Abraham (as is done in the prayer *Supra quae propitio)* is an insult to Christ, for it is his sacrifice alone that sanctifies theirs.[39]

Luther's second objection concerns the petition that God would vouchsafe to accept the body and blood of Christ as a sacrifice.[40]

[35] *WA* 18, 25, 27; 15, 767.

[36] *Te igitur* reads in part: "vouchsafe to receive and bless these gifts, these offerings, these holy and unblemished sacrifices which in the first place we offer for Thy holy Catholic Church," and *Hanc igitur:* "This oblation therefore of our service . . . we beseech Thee, O Lord, graciously to accept" (*ut placatus accipias*).

[37] *Quam oblationem* reads in part, "Which oblation do Thou, O God, vouchsafe in all things to bless, approve, ratify, make worthy and acceptable; that it may become for us the Body and Blood of Thy most beloved Son, our Lord Jesus Christ."

[38] Luther often noted the very confused train of thought in these prayers and concluded that they had been compiled by an unlearned monk (*WA* TR 4, 606). The other places where Luther refers to the author of the Canon are: *WA* 18, 27, 28; 15, 768; 8, 449; 12, 207.

[39] *WA* 18, 30.

[40] For example the prayer *Supra quae propitio* reads in part: ". . . vouchsafe to look on them with a propitious and serene countenance and to receive

This seems to imply that Christ is unholy and unclean in himself and that he needs the prayers of men in order to become a sacrifice acceptable to God.[41] Man makes himself the mediator between God and Christ.[42] If that is not the height of blasphemy, what is?[43]

Surely we can understand Luther's revulsion at the whole tenor and spirit of the Canon prayers.[44] These were the prayers which rated higher than the work of Christ himself, for they were thought absolutely essential to make his sacrifice acceptable before God. But in reality, they made a mockery of the whole Christian religion.

Originally, Luther permitted the Canon prayers to be read before the consecration, with the understanding that they referred to the earthly gifts only or to the sacrifice of prayer.[45] But ultimately, he realized that it was impossible to tolerate the Canon and abolished it completely.[46] Outwardly this may look like pure destructiveness. Actually it was a necessary step in order to restore the original purpose and meaning of the mass.

Thus we have contrasted the two concepts of worship for which Luther used the terms *beneficium* and *sacrificium.* The one refers to the worship of the true church, the other to the idolatry of the

them. . . . ." and the concluding prayer *Placeat tibi* ". . . that the sacrifice may be acceptable to Thee. . . ."

[41] *WA* 18, 30; 18, 36: "The dear Christ is not acceptable with the Father without St. Canon to make him acceptable so that the sacrifice might atone for him before God."

[42] *WA* 18, 30: "There he is praying again for the sacrifice that God would be gracious towards his Son and be pleased with him. Miserable man makes himself a mediator between God and Christ, his dear Son."

[43] *WA* 18, 28: "God is sure to be pleased if I pray he should grant my petition and begin to have mercy on his Son."

[44] *WA* 6, 365, 375, 522.

[45] *WA* 6, 524.

[46] *WA* 8, 448: "Yield to the gospel, O Canon, and give room to the Holy Spirit, since thou art merely a human word."

pseudo-church. We have traced this contrast point by point and now we summarize the result of our inquiry as follows: Worship is the gift of the gracious God through the incarnate and suffering Christ for his congregation which receives the gift by faith and so enters into fellowship with God. Thus worship is a participation in the work of Christ.

Two questions remain: What is the gift given by God in worship? And what is meant by participating through faith in worship? We shall answer these questions by describing worship as the work of God and as the work of faith.

WORSHIP AS THE WORK OF GOD

3

The Proclamation of the Word

Holy Scripture is the one and only foundation of Luther's theology of worship. This fact is vital.[1] He countered the ingenious allegorical expositions of the mass of the Middle Ages not with any theological constructions of his own, but with the witness of Scripture.[2]

A Free Course for the Word

Luther's greatest concern in the reform of worship was the restoration of the Word to its rightful place. In his pamphlet of 1523, "On the Order of Public Worship," he calls the neglect of the Word the worst abuse of medieval worship.[3] "This is the sum of the matter. Let everything be done so that the Word may have free course instead of the prattling and rattling that has been the rule up to now. We can spare everything except the Word. Again we profit by nothing as much as by the Word. For the whole Scripture shows that the Word should have free course among Christians. And in Luke 10 [v. 42], Christ himself says: 'One thing is needful,' namely, that Mary sit at the feet of Christ and hear his Word daily. This is the best part to choose which shall not be taken away for ever. It is an eternal Word. Everything else must pass away, no matter how much care and trouble

[1] See, for example, *WA* 6, 355ff; 8, 431ff; 11, 432.

[2] *WA* 6, 526: "Those who now explain the mass toy and trifle with allegorizing human ceremonies."

[3] *WA* 12, 35: "Three great abuses have befallen worship. The first is that God's Word was muffled and reading and singing alone were left in the churches. This is the worst abuse."

it may give to Martha. To this God help us. Amen."[4] What is implied in this demand? This is not the place to discuss Luther's theology of the Word in all its ramifications. But we must try to understand the role in worship of the Word of God and the meaning of the term "proclamation of the Word."[5]

In *De Servo Arbitrio* Luther has made the well-known distinction between the hidden and the revealed God.[6] God in his majesty is hidden and inaccessible to man. We cannot find or see him as he is. But he has condescended to take the form of the Word, born in Bethlehem, and proclaimed in the world. As such he is revealed to man. And as such we can know him and have fellowship with him.

This distinction throws light on the meaning of the Word of God in worship. The God we preach and worship is not the hidden one but he who revealed himself in his Word.[7] To hear and believe the Word is therefore worship at its truest and best.[8]

At times Luther stressed the distinction between God in himself and in his Word.[9] Since the incarnation, the Word belongs on the side of created things. God will allow no other access to himself except through the incarnate Word Jesus Christ.[10] It is in Christ that he wants to be found. And the words "Hear ye him" (Matt. 17:5) indicate the one and only approach to God.[11] But this distinction between God and his Word implies no separation. The Word is God,[12] not only the eternal, uncreated, pre-existing

[4] *WA* 12, 37.

[5] Compare the following works for Luther's theology of the Word: K. Thieme, *Luthers Stellung zur heiligen Schrift* (Guetersloh: 1903); R. Prenter, *op. cit.*, pp. 101-130.

[6] *WA* 18, 685. [7] *WA* 42, 634. [8] *WA* 40^{I}, 130, 361.

[9] *WA* 18, 606: "God and the Scripture of God are two things, just as the Creator and the creature are two things."

[10] Erich Seeberg, *Luthers Theologie* (Stuttgart: 1937), II, p. 393.

[11] *WA* 39^{I}, 391. [12] *WA* 12, 107, 300.

Word (John 1:1), but also the incarnate, created, and revealed Word. In all its earthly lowliness, the Word brings God to man.[13] In this sense, Luther's entire theology is a theology of the Word.

Christ himself is the Word. In essence he is one with God (hence Luther's identification of God and the Word). But at the same time he is the second person of the Godhead, incarnate and revealed in the world of creation (hence Luther's distinction of the Word and God). In Luther's theology of the Word, the Word must always be understood christocentrically.

All this goes to show that Luther's concern was with the Word as a means of revelation. He refused to speculate on the eternal Word. To him, the Word and its proclamation were the weapons by which God subdues his enemies and frees mankind from bondage.[14] This cosmic warfare began with the incarnation. And it continues after Christ's death and resurrection in spite of the victory which he obtained. The Word written and preached is the sword with which he pursues his struggle up to the Last Day.

Aside from this war, the Word cannot be understood. It always lays its hearer under obligation, addresses him, arrests him, condemns and comforts him. But it escapes the one who tries to listen in cool detachment.[15] One cannot hear the message at a safe distance outside its perimeter. It speaks to us of our own existence, our own battle with sin and death. If we try to remain neutral, we have already deserted.

[13] *WA* 10 I, 1, 188: "God's Word is so fully equal to him that his whole Godhead is in it, and he who has the Word, has the whole Godhead."

[14] *WA* 30 II, 621: "God's Word must have no mean enemies but the mightiest ones, so as to prove its power in defeating them. Such are these four companions: the flesh, the world, death, and the devil. This is why Christ is named the Lord Sabaoth, i.e. a God of hosts or of warfare, who is always at war and contends within us."

[15] A. Allwohn, *op. cit.*, p. 121; G. Wingren, *Predikan* (Lund: 1949), p. 20ff. *WA* 31I, 67.

Luther's demand that the Word have free course implies the wish that the warfare of Christ through the Word might dominate and mold the church service. His views about Christ's rule through the Word are deeply revelant to his picture of worship.

The Word and the Works of God

The Word reveals the works of God, past, present, and future. It is not a philosophy, but a message, not a flight into the realm of fancy, but a witness to the works which God does for us men and in this our world. Without the Word, the works remain meaningless.[16]

The great facts of our salvation are more than historical events. They escape objective observation, for they make a personal claim on every man. This claim comes through the Word. The Word transforms the "then" into a "now." It renders the past relevant to the present. It makes Christ the contemporary of every generation.

Of course, both creation and redemption are completed acts of God.[17] God has left nothing undone in his dealings with mankind. But the Holy Ghost must make the works of God available for the benefit of men. "Creation has been finished. Our redemption has been accomplished too. But until the Last Day the Holy Spirit continues his work unceasingly, for which he appoints a congregation on earth by which he says and does everything."[18] He bridges the chasm between the past works of God and men living today, for men cannot appropriate the works of God by their own reason and strength. It is just here

[16] *WA* 10 I, 1, 131: "For if the life and suffering of Christ had not been comprehended in the Word to which faith might cling, it would have been of no value; for all those who saw it with their own eyes received no or very little benefit." 10 I, 2, 203: "If he had not begun to preach, his birth would have had no value."

[17] *WA* 30 I, 188.

[18] *WA* 30 I, 191.

that the theology of the mass according to the Roman church and the spiritualism of the Enthusiasts failed. Both would replace the function of the Holy Spirit by the works of man; the Roman church by the sacrifice of the mass, and the Enthusiasts by the "inner light."

But their attempts are futile and unnecessary. God himself imparts the benefits of his redemptive work through the Holy Spirit. "Neither you nor I could ever know anything of Christ or believe in him and have him for our Lord except as it is offered to us by the Holy Spirit through the preaching of the gospel."[19] Our present age, no less than past or future, is part of redemptive history.

This explains why Luther stressed the preaching of Christ's birth, death, and resurrection more than these historical events proper.[20] The Word alone conveys the truth that all the works of God are done for our benefit. It was not Christ who needed to be saved, but we. Our adoption by God, our dying to sin, our righteousness are included in his birth, death, and resurrection.

"God did not want to make Christ known to the world other than through his Word, and by thus spreading knowledge of him abroad he offers him to everyone. Otherwise Christ would have remained isolated and unknown to us. He would therefore have died only for and by himself. As the Word bears Christ, so the Word bears us to him who has vanquished death, sin, and devil."[21]

By this Luther did not mean to deny the historical validity of Christ's life and death. They are the beginning of a chain re-

[19] *WA* 30 I, 188. Cf. 26, 296.

[20] *WA* 10 I, 2, 7; 12, 260; 34 I, 318. Cf. *WA* Bibel 6, 10. This distinction between the work of redemption and its use (*Gebrauch*) explains the fact that Luther preferred the Epistles to the Gospels (*WA* 12, 260).

[21] *WA* 17 II, 234. Cf. 23, 189.

action which includes God's works among his people today. They are the warranty for the benefits which we now receive.[22]

Occasionally, Luther distinguished between the fact and the use of the fact *(factum* and *usus facti),* and between merit and the distribution of the merit *(meritum* and *distributio meriti).*[23] The work of Christ *(factum* and *meritum)* and the work of the Holy Spirit through the Word *(usus)* must not be considered separately. Luther included the church (the Word, use, and distribution) in the historical work of Christ.

With this perspective he resolved the dilemma of the so-called objective and subjective theories of redemption. The objective view tends to isolate Christ's work of redemption from those for whom he died and rose. The subjective view considers his work an event of the past and stresses the personal psychological appropriation of it. But Luther saw past and present merely as different phases of redemptive history. The present is the era of the Holy Spirit who through the Word brings Christ to all the nations. Thus the use of the fact is nothing but God's continued work in its application to mankind, and the sermon nothing less than redemptive history revealed in the Word.[24]

This unity of work and word rests on the dual nature of Christ.[25] Christ was true man, born of the Virgin. He bore the curse of the law and the guilt of mankind. But he suffered and died vicariously, for he was without sin. Therefore his cross concerned, not him, but those whose sins he bore. Only in his

[22] G. Wingren, *Predikan,* p. 150, 165ff.

[23] *WA* 26, 40, 296, 506; 18, 203; 30[I], 188.

[24] *WA* 29, 200 (Roerer): "If Christ had been crucified a hundred times, but no one proclaimed it, the remission of sins would be lost. Thus this work which was wrought on the cross must be revealed in the Word and through the Word be offered to the people."

[25] Suffice it here to refer the reader to the classical exposition of Luther's teaching on redemption in his exegesis of Galatians 3:13, in the Large Commentary on Galatians (especially *WA* 40 [I], 432-441).

solidarity with sinful mankind was he a sinner, not in himself. As such he suffered the wrath of God. But because he was both God and man in one person, the battle became a mighty struggle in his own person. This struggle was fought, not for his sake, nor as a contest between God and the devil, but in order to free man from the devil's domination.[26] Thus the opposition between the curse (wrath) of God and his eternal blessing (love) is not a conflict between different attributes of God, but a definition of man's concrete existence. For in Christ God deals with mankind. And his victory derives from the fact that Christ is not only man but God and man at the same time. The victory was attained not for his benefit but for ours. For it is the very nature of God to give himself for others. Thus mankind shares vicariously in the triumph of Christ over sin, death, and the devil.[27]

In that Christ's redemptive work is for us it implies the message of the Word. For it is the nature of the message to be directed to us and be valid for us as the divine work. To preach is more than to report and comment on certain events of the past. It is to make Christ our contemporary so that his death and resurrection become our own[28] and the redemption which he wrought becomes our righteousness. Indeed, one cannot accurately describe the work of Christ without reference to the people for whom he died and rose again.[29]

[26] This explains Luther's vigorous stress on the vicarious character of Christ's work of redemption; *WA* 40 I, 437.

[27] [Here the author inserts a critique of the so-called "classical" theory of redemption, as championed by Bishop Aulén in his well-known book *Christus Victor*. Our translation omits this section. Trans.]

[28] *WA* 17 I, 96 (Roerer).

[29] *WA* 17 I, 72 (Roerer): "There is a difference between proclaiming the passion of Christ and its appropriation. The devil does the former, the Holy Ghost the latter." Cf. 86 (Roerer) and 29, 271 (Roerer): "Wherever you read: He arose, there continue: I with him, you with him, so that that resurrection may be drawn into us and we into it. Not to learn this is to learn nothing."

Christ's work of redemption does not cancel the twofold aspect of God's dealings with mankind. He continues to deal with us in love or in wrath. For Christ's work does not imply the resolution of a conflict between differing attributes of God, as though God's love had overcome his wrath. Then the Word of reconciliation would simply mean the victory of God's love. But the work of redemption is much more than a process in the mind of God. It is an act of God. God acted when he reconciled the world in Jesus Christ. Christ has borne vicariously the sins of all mankind and suffered for their sake the wrath of God. By striking him, God's wrath struck all mankind. So the word of Jesus' death is a word of condemnation (law). The voice of condemnation in the law forces all men into the fellowship of the death of Christ. Christ's continued work of redemption makes us die with him, for we stand condemned by the fact of his death for our sins. But he who submits to the verdict of the law submits to the wrath of God as did Christ. He belongs to the Crucified and therefore also to the Risen One. In the midst of death he receives life. To raise us with Christ is the proper work of God, or, as it were, the proper Word of God—the gospel.

Thus the law and the gospel remain the twofold message of the Christian pulpit.[30] Far from being principles of human conduct, they are the dealings of God in Christ with mankind. They cannot be divorced either from the historical events of the past or from the situation of the present-day listener. The wrath of God and his love, the law and the gospel cannot be described objectively *(an sich)*, but only as the expression of actual fellowship with God.

Thus the proclamation of Christ's work is in itself an integral part of his work. The Word explains the work. And the work

[30] *WA* 7, 52; 10 I, 2, 155; and 49, 652 (Roerer).

bears no fruit without the Word. The devil is unabashed by Christ's death and resurrection as mere facts of the past. He is quite content to have people accept these events as part of ancient history. What he opposes is the preaching of the Word which would apply them to men in their need. By my own reason and strength I can indeed learn and accept the story of Christ. But I cannot see the hand of God in it[31] until the Word reveals it to me and kindles my faith.[32] As long as it remains "that sweet story of old," it is the teaching of men (or rather of the devil). It must become my own story in order to be truly the Word of God. But the conflict between the teaching of men and the Word of God is only one aspect of the struggle between Christ and the devil and will continue to the Last Day.[33]

Scripture and Pulpit

In the conflict between the Word of God and the teaching of men, Holy Scripture plays a decisive part. Luther found the Word of God in the Bible. Biblical lessons were to replace the "un-Christian fables and lies" which had usurped their place in the church.[34] But he demanded more than lessons from the Bible. To him "using Scripture" was not tantamount to "reading Scripture." It implied the preaching of the Word by which the redemptive facts of the Bible could be applied to the congregation.

It is possible to misinterpret Scripture. The divine nature of the Word is as hidden in the Bible as it was in the manger of

[31] *WA* 29, 273: "That Christ had risen was most certainly a true fact. Yet when the disciples and the women followed their reason alone they concluded, 'They have taken away the Lord.' Behold what reason does, even when the fact is open to the eye. Without the Word, the tomb certainly remains empty."

[32] *WA* 17 II, 132; 23, 189; 26, 569; 370 (Roerer; cf. also the print); 51, 286.

[33] *WA* 18, 627.

[34] *WA* 12, 35; cf. 17 II, 208, 209.

Bethlehem or on the cross of Calvary. Faith is needed to find the Word of God in the Bible.

As the unbelieving Jews refused to acknowledge the sonship of Jesus, so modern unbelief fails to find the Word of God in the Bible. This is the work of the devil. Men read their own preconceived ideas into the Bible[35] and draw from it heresies instead of the truth. "I have observed that all heresies and misunderstanding of Scriptures are caused not, as is commonly alleged, by the simplicity of its language, but by the fact that people neglect the simple, plain meaning of the words and affect tropes and figures of speech of their own invention."[36]

Man has an inner resistance to the truth which must be broken by Christ. The correct understanding of Scripture is a gift of the Lord, and it comes to men, not through an inner light, but through serious study of the text.[37] The Bible has to be interpreted, not because it lacks clarity, but because men lack perceptiveness. Far from understanding spiritual matters, they don't even master the linguistic problems.[38] Scripture does not yield its meaning without meditation. And meditation implies a careful study of the text. It requires not only contemplation but painstaking philological research. Yet there is nothing purely objective about this research. Bible study is an intensely personal matter. For it aims at blocking the "static" of man's own misconceptions that the voice of God in the Bible might be heard.[39]

Thus the difficulty in interpreting the Bible has nothing to do with an alleged discrepancy between its content and its form. The interpreter has no call to separate the chaff from the wheat or to search for so-called "deeper truths" behind the plain "external" word of Scripture. For the problem of interpretation

[35] *WA* 40 II, 36. [36] *WA* 18, 701. [37] *WA* 18, 163.
[38] *WA* 18, 606, 659. [39] R. Prenter, *op. cit.* (English), pp. 114ff.

is not a problem of the book, but one of the interpreter.[40] If the message of the Bible concerned anything less than his total existence, there would be no problem of exegesis. This serves to explain why Luther clung to certain words of Scripture and rejected any evasion of the plain sense of the words. The plain sense of words was to him the only effective bar against misinterpretation.

The text as such was not problematical to him. He asked not: What is in the Bible? but: What does this mean to me? For the same reason he insisted that the oral proclamation or preaching is the proper form of the Word. Originally, the gospel was not a book but a sermon,[41] and the church not a *Federhaus* (quill house), but a *Mundhaus* (mouth house).[42] The crystallization of the gospel in a book was prompted by the rise of heresies, and therefore indirectly by the power of sin.[43] But Christ never wrote anything, and his apostles were not scribes but messengers. So today the Bible must be preached if the gospel is to assume its proper form and fulfil its proper task.

The pulpit stands between the lectern and the pew. It applies the Bible truths of old to the congregation of today. It is in the sermon that the letter which kills becomes the Spirit which gives life.[44] Thus Scripture and sermon stand in the same relation to each other as the work and the Word of God (compare the last section). And as the Word does not impair the validity of the works of God, so the sermon does not impinge on the importance of the Bible. After all the Bible itself witnesses to the importance

[40] Karl Barth's tendency to distinguish between the word of man and the Word of God within Scripture is foreign to Luther's view. Luther rather pursues the theme of a war between God and the devil as men use the Scriptures. For a critique of Barth's doctrine of the Word, see Bengt-E. Benktson, *Den naturliga teologiens problem hos Karl Barth* (Lund: 1948), p. 193ff, 268ff.

[41] *WA* 10 I, 1, 17; 10 I, 1, 626; 12, 259.

[42] *WA* 10 I, 2, 48; 7, 475.

[43] *WA* 10 I, 1, 627; 10 I, 1, 14; 7, 526.

[44] *WA* 10 I, 2, 35; 7, 475.

of the oral gospel in the early church. The sermon does not supersede Scripture but "uses" it. Here is the main emphasis in Luther's concept of Scripture. He is interested in the message of the Bible, not in theories about its origin or form. He sees in the Bible not a document the validity of which needed to be examined or proven, but a message concerning man and his existence. The first issue may get passing notice, but in comparison with the latter it is trivial and inconsequential.

The Pulpit as the Battlefield of Christ

Rarely did Luther preach without a text. And even his textless sermons are, in a wider sense, expositions of Scripture. Ordinarily he expounded a definite lesson or part of it, on Sundays and feast days the lesson for the day, on weekdays successive chapters of a given book of Scripture. Nor did he try to extract a theme from his text. His one and only subject is Christ and all his sermons are variations on this great theme, for to him the sermon was Christ's continued "advent," his coming to every generation of men, the means by which he establishes fellowship with his own.[45] One could also say that righteousness is the continual subject of Luther's preaching, that is, the righteousness which Christ obtained and which he offers to men through the preaching of the Word.[46] Every sermon should vindicate the justification of faith against the justification by works.

It was this christocentric emphasis that Luther missed in the Roman church. The Christ of the Roman pulpit was not the Christ of the gospel but a stern judge of men's works or an example to be imitated.[47] He inspired fear rather than comfort.[48]

Luther saw the difference between the sort of proclamation

[45] *WA* 10 I, 1, 13; 40 I, 537.
[46] *WA* 10 I, 1, 19.
[47] *WA* 10 I, 2, 112; 10 I, 1, 9.
[48] *WA* 12, 265.

that he wanted and the preaching of the pseudo-church as a conflict of legalistic and evangelical preaching. The preachers of the pope's church had failed to present Christ as a gift to men.[49] They had turned the gospel into law, or—what amounts to the same thing—had confused the two. "Those who interpret the word gospel other than as 'good news' do not understand it at all, as do those who make it a law instead of grace and give us Moses instead of Christ."[50]

This is why he began his collection of sermons *(Kirchenpostille)* with a brief instruction on what one should seek and expect in the Gospels. He explains the above-mentioned difference in regard to the person and office of Christ.[51] Christ is no more a model to be imitated than any other saint. He is not truly known until he is accepted by faith as our Saviour. Every sermon must present him as God's gift "for us."

In order to offer the true message of Christ, the preacher must be able to distinguish properly between gospel and law.[52] For redemptive history can be seen either under the aspect of the law or from the viewpoint of the gospel. The former view falsifies the message of Scripture. Christ becomes a lawgiver. Grace becomes a virtue by which man is supposed to recommend himself to God. Christ's sufferings and death become an example to be followed by the faithful. But this imitation of the dying and rising Christ is a purely human endeavor. And it amounts to a complete perversion of the biblical way of salvation.

The evangelical understanding of Scripture leads to a totally different approach. Christ's death and resurrection should be

[49] *WA* 10 I, 1, 10.
[50] *WA* 56, 338. See also *WA* 10 I, 1, 419.
[51] *WA* 10 I, 1, 8ff.
[52] *WA* 10 I, 2, 155.

represented not as a pattern to be imitated, but as a present reality proclaimed and offered in the Word. Both God's wrath over sin (the punishment) and his life-giving love preclude human works, for they are the marks of God's dealing in Christ with men. Through the Word of the law and of the gospel we are drawn into the redemptive work of Christ.

Thus the evangelical aspect does not impair the twofold nature of the Word (law and gospel, death and resurrection). But it speaks of the law (death) as fulfilled and overcome by Christ. The proper understanding of this distinction between the law and the gospel is the foremost task of the preacher. The legalistic pulpit confuses the two, the evangelical pulpit keeps them "undivided" and "unconfused."[53] Luther's own sermons illustrate this distinction. Their focus is always the work of Christ.[54] This is the central message which he found in every text. On the other hand, from this central position he felt free to criticize certain books or selections of the Bible.[55] He questioned the apostolic origin of the Epistle of James because it fails to witness to the resurrection of Christ. From the same viewpoint he evaluated other books of the Bible.[56] He deplored the one-sided emphasis in the epistle lessons of the church year. It offered too many parenetic sections

[53] *WA* 7, 504ff.

[54] The literature about Luther's own sermons is very scanty. Of newer works we mention the chapter in Y. Brilioth, *Predikans historia* (Lund: 1945), p. 93ff, as well as the literature quoted there.

[55] For Luther's use of the church year lessons see especially Gustav Lindberg, *Kyrkans heliga år* (Stockholm: 1937), p. 353ff. For Luther's attitude toward the Canon see K. Holl, *Gesammelte Aufsaetze,* I, p. 561.

[56] *WA* 12, 268: "From this one can tell true Christian teaching and preaching, for to preach the gospel, one must preach the resurrection of Christ. Whoever fails to preach this is no apostle, for this is the crown of our faith. And the noblest and best books are those which teach and treat the resurrection the most. Thus it can easily be seen that the Epistle of St. James is not a proper apostolic epistle." Cf. *WA* Bibel 6, 10, 23; 7, 384.

instead of those which teach the righteousness of faith.[57] However he made no changes but preached on the prescribed lessons with a clear evangelical emphasis.[58]

The Place of the Sermon in Worship.

When Luther demanded the proclamation of the Word, he was thinking of two forms of worship: the office (canonical hours) and the mass.[59] With the Reformation the canonical hours became daily services, while the mass became the order of worship for Sundays and holy days. Luther insisted on the sermon in both forms. Even in the canonical hours he was not content with the mere reading of the Word without an exposition.[60] Actually, this was not a matter of principle with him,[61] but resulted from the abuses which he sought to correct, namely the fact that legends of the saints had enjoyed equal rank with the Bible in the calendar of pericopes, and the fact that even the reading of Scripture had become a work of merit. Long chapters were faithfully read from the lectern, but without aid from the pulpit, people failed to find the Word in the words. He therefore combined reading and preaching, even as Paul had placed interpretation with speaking in tongues.[62]

As for the mass, preaching was no innovation. It had been quite common during the Middle Ages.[63] Yet the sermon gained new stature through the Reformation. Before, it was optional.

[57] *WA* 12, 209.

[58] *WA* 19, 95.

[59] See, for example, *Von Ordnung des Gottesdiensts* (1523).

[60] *WA* 12, 35.

[61] R. Prenter, *Spiritus Creator* (1944), p. 151, n. 106 (German), stresses the fact that the Word can also be "proclamation" when read. For the same reason, Luther appreciated the biblical lessons as a treasure which had been preserved even under the pope (*WA* 38, 221, 231; 46, 624).

[62] *WA* 12, 35.

[63] Y. Brilioth, *op. cit.*, p. 77ff, 83ff.

It lacked an organic relation to the mass. The best that could be said of medieval preaching is that it sought to direct the people to the benefits of the mass by expounding the law.[64] But it remained for Luther to recover the early Christian co-ordination of sermon and sacrament.

Luther proceeded from the Words of Institution. "When the Lord instituted the mass, he said, 'This do in remembrance of me,' as though he meant to say, 'As oft as you do this sacrament, you shall preach of me.' "[65] The difference between Luther and the Middle Ages lies in the exegesis of I Corinthians 11:26. The medieval "remembrance" consisted in a dramatical representation of the passion of Christ. But to Luther, the sermon itself was the remembrance and he quoted Luke 22:19, Psalm 102:21, and Psalm 111:4f in support of his exegesis.[66] This concept of remembrance is found in as early a work as his first commentary on the psalter. Here he quotes I Corinthians 11:26 as a proof for the connection between the gospel (in this connection probably a lesson in the mass) and the Sacrament.[67] In later years it was an understanding which he took for granted.[68]

Luther identified the remembrance with the sermon because he understood the remembrance as a part of God's redemptive work, rather than as a work of man.[69] Compare his exposition of Psalm 111:5, "He will ever be mindful of his covenant":

"Furthermore, in the Sacrament we keep the remembrance of his covenant according to Christ's institution. For it is not our own institution or work but his. He performs it through us and

[64] R. Seeberg, *Lehrbuch der Dogmengeschichte,* III, p. 413f.
[65] *WA* 6, 373.
[66] For example *WA* 1, 204, 334, 444, 604; 4, 236, 610, etc.
[67] *WA* 4, 236.
[68] *WA* 6, 359; 12, 180; 19, 505.
[69] *WA* 12, 181.

in us; for he is speaking not of the inward remembering in the heart, but of the outward, public, and oral remembering to which Christ referred when he said: This do in remembrance of me—which is done through the sermon and the Word of God."[70] This exegesis leads logically on to the next verse: "He hath showed his people the power of his works" (Psalm 111:6); for it links the elements of proclamation and of remembrance.

This idea of remembrance differs markedly from that of the Enthusiasts. They understood remembrance as an inner effort on the part of man, an ascent of the individual soul to God.[71] Luther called this a remembrance *im Winkel* (in one's own private corner),[72] for here the individual was expected to secure his own tryst with God, apart from the congregation.[73]

The bond between sermon and Sacrament was further strengthened by Luther's definition of the sermon as an exposition of the mass.[74] He implied not the explanation of the liturgy as had been customary during the Middle Ages, but rather the evangelical scope of the sermon. To him, the "mass" was the New Testament as instituted by Christ.[75] Here he found the message of Christ's redemptive work on our behalf, the word of the cross, in short, the whole gospel in a nutshell.[76] To find and expound this theme in every text was the principal task of the preacher, and any sermon which presented the alternative of the gospel versus the law, of the righteousness of faith versus the righteousness of works, of Christ versus the devil was a proper exposition of the mass.

[70] *WA* 31 I, 417. [71] *WA* 30 II, 609. [72] *WA* 19, 505.
[73] *WA* 31 I, 417. [74] *WA* 6, 231; 6, 526. [75] *WA* 6, 373f.
[76] *WA* 6, 374. This is the reason why, in the *Deutsche Messe,* the Words of Institution are to be chanted to the same tune as the Gospel (*WA* 19, 197); compare the editor's preface to the *Deutsche Messe* in *WA* 19, 59; Theodor Knolle, *Die Eucharistiefeier und der lutherische Gottesdienst* (Erlangen: 1939), p. 11f.

4

The Presence of Christ in the Lord's Supper

Luther defines the presence of God in a twofold sense. First he speaks of God's omnipresence and second of his presence in the incarnate Christ, in the church, and in the service. These two modes of his presence must be carefully kept apart.

Omnipresence and Presence-for-us

God is present everywhere.[1] As the Creator he is above his creation and its limitations. He can be present at once in the smallest creature and fill all the earth,[2] for he is not identical with what he made. He would be man and not God if he could be comprehended in the categories of his creation. Otherwise he would be an object for the experience and reason of man. But the "natural" presence of God is not a conclusion of "natural" theology. It is an article of faith. "God has two modes of being present. One is natural, the other spiritual. His natural presence reaches everywhere, as Isaiah says in the 66th chapter (v.1): 'The heaven is my throne, and the earth is my footstool.' Thus he is also in the midst of hell, death, and sins, as says the psalm quoted above (139:8): 'If I make my bed in hell, behold, thou

[1] *WA* 28, 141. The following passages are the ones which Luther quotes most frequently in this connection: Ps. 139:7f; Jer. 23:23; Isa. 66:1; Acts 17:27.

[2] *WA* 26, 339: "God is not a spatial being, long, wide, thick, high, or deep, but a supernatural, unsearchable being, which could be at once in a little seed and yet be present in and above and beyond all creatures." Cf. 26, 340.

art there.' No one can escape him. But he is spiritually present only where he is known, where his Word, faith, Spirit, and worship are found; here are his own who realize that God is a mighty Lord who is omnipotent and present everywhere."[3]

God's omnipresence is shared by Christ. The Son has had all the attributes of the Father from eternity. By his incarnation and exaltation he lost none of them, but imparted them to his human nature.[4]

As the one at the right hand of God, he fills heaven and earth with the glory, for he shares the omnipresence of the Creator.[5]

The omnipresence of God and Christ reflects the majesty of the divine nature and its sovereignty over the world of creation. God's mode of being present far transcends the ways in which his creatures can be present. It suits his nature. That is why Luther calls it a "natural presence."

As the Omnipresent, God is inescapable. There is no neutral sphere beyond his reach. This assures the believer of the all-inclusive love of God. But it also strikes fear into the breast of the unbeliever who resents the reach of God. Face to face with an ever-present God, he suffers the pangs of a restless conscience. A "shaken leaf" will frighten him, for in his wickedness, all things speak to him of an angry God.[6]

[3] *WA* 19, 197.

[4] *WA* 23, 147. For the doctrine of ubiquity see Paul W. Gennrich, *Die Christologie Luthers im Abendmahlsstreit* (Koenigsberg: 1929), p. 140ff.

[5] *WA* 23, 145: "He is at the right hand of God, which means nothing else but that even as a man he is above all things, has all things under himself and reigns over them." 23, 153: "It agrees with Scripture and faith that the body of Christ is at once in heaven and in the Lord's Supper. And properly, it derives from the First Article where it says: 'I believe in God the Father Almighty, Maker of heaven and earth.' "

[6] *WA* 19, 226f; 1, 74; 23, 133; 19, 226. See Rudolf Johannesson, *Person och gemenskap enligt Romersk-katolsk och luthersk grundåslådning* (Lund: 1947), p. 223. The expression "shaken leaf" comes from Leviticus 26:36 which Luther usually quoted in this connection.

Thus, though present everywhere, God remains invisible to sinful man. Nowhere except in Christ can he be found or seen,[7] for Christ alone is "true God and true man." The personal union makes it possible for man to see God in the man Jesus. Christ is the only way to God. Seeking God anywhere else, one finds not him, but the devil.[8] For the devil wants to divide the divine from the human nature of Christ and to persuade men to seek a direct approach to God.[9]

The fact that Christ was made subject to the law, became man, and, as a man, contended against sin, wrath, and the devil, explains the hidden nature of his kingdom, for the gospel remains hidden under the law, the divine under the human nature, the victory of Christ under the struggle which is still being fought. And those who refuse to acknowledge this hiddenness of Christ's revelation are bound to confuse the law and the gospel and so to confirm the wrath of God.

God indeed is present everywhere, but he cannot be found everywhere, at least not as the God of love and mercy. There is a significant difference between his omnipresence and his "presence-for-us." The latter is a presence in the Word. God can be found only where he adds the Word to his work. Otherwise he is not present-for-us, though we must believe his presence as that of the Creator.[10] Christ's presence in the Word explains another term used by Luther in this connection: the "spiritual presence."[11] Here "spiritual" must not be equated with "immaterial" (in the sense of Greek philosophy) for the presence in question is that of the incarnate Christ. "Spiritual" refers to material realities of this world insofar as they are "comprehended in God's Word" and accepted in faith. Wherever Word and faith are, there also

[7] *WA* 23, 151. [8] *WA* 28, 119. [9] *WA* 28, 118.
[10] *WA* 19, 492; 23, 149, 151. [11] *WA* 19, 197.

is the Holy Spirit prompting our faith to apply the Word to the realities of this world. The most ordinary and earthly things of this world become spiritual realities when by faith they have been linked with the Word of God.

"Whatever is done outwardly in the body, when God's Word comes in and it is done in faith, becomes a spiritual work. Nothing can be so physical, carnal, or outward that it would not become spiritual when it proceeds through the Word and faith."[12]

God's presence in the Word is not limited to the earthly ministry of Christ. It continues to the present age. From the ascension on, Christ has been active through the Holy Spirit. He has power over all creation and can choose certain media to convey the Spirit's gifts. Thus his human nature has been freed for wider reach and influence. His ministry in the flesh was limited to Jewish soil. But now his mission and his work reach to the ends of the earth.[13]

He has not left the earth, as the Enthusiasts claimed, but is present according to his human nature wherever the Word prevails. "Even now the kingdom of Christ is here in power. Now he speaks the Word, and through it rules over devil, sin, death, and all things by his humanity. On the Last Day it will be revealed. Thus, while God rules always, it is not apparent to us. He sees us but we do not see him."[14] Of course, his life in the body is a matter of the past. Yet he is present in the outward and material world. Otherwise the world would be left to the devil.[15]

His redemptive warfare goes on in the world as his Word is preached and the sacraments granted. Thus fallen man is led back to the gifts of creation. He is returned to, not removed from the earth. For it was the devil who diverted man from the earth

[12] *WA* 23, 189. Cf. n. 11 above. Salvation might depend on lifting a straw if God had so decreed. See for example *WA* 10 I, 1, 310; 24, 254; etc.

[13] *WA* 10 I, 1, 21.
[14] *WA* 14, 28.
[15] *WA* 28, 141.

where God is to an imaginary heaven where he is not. He prompted man to seek God per se *(an sich)* instead of within his earthly existence. But it is here that God contends for the salvation and redemption of man. He does not sit on his throne in splendid isolation from the troubles of this earth but shares them in Christ. This is his glory which is not in the least impaired by Christ's presence in earthly things. The Enthusiasts objected to this presence and sought to obtain the Holy Spirit on their own. But God comes to man through things material. And this presence calls for faith.[16]

The spiritual presence of God through the Word and faith is realized in worship. Through the proclamation of the Word and the administration of the sacraments, God creates the only proper form of worship—faith. His presence cannot be divorced from the church service. Because he is on the right hand of the Father, Christ can be found in the Word and in the sacraments.[17]

Luther's picture of the twofold presence of God reflects the leading lines of his theology. His distinction of omnipresence and presence-for-us recalls his idea of the hidden God, for within the hidden God he distinguished between "God in himself" and "God for us." The first term refers to God's hiddenness in his majesty, the second to his hiddenness in Christ, the hiddenness of revelation. The one recalls the natural presence of "God in himself," the latter God's presence in Christ, that is "for us" in Word and sacrament. God's omnipresence reflects the majesty and sovereignty which the hiddenness of God implies in the experience of men.

There is a certain parallel between the omnipresence and the omnipotence of God. Omnipresence implies that God is present even in the devil and in hell,[18] while omnipotence implies that

[16] *WA* 28, 576. [17] *WA* 28, 143. [18] *WA* 19, 197, 219.

he is also driving Satan in his wickedness and men in their work righteousness.[19] Thus the omnipresence and omnipotence of God belong in the same theological framework—that of his majestic hiddenness. The fact of his omnipresence and omnipotence rests on the witness of Scripture. But even so, it is a truth not to analyze but to worship in awe,[20] for though omnipresent, God remains unapproachable in his majesty until that day when "I shall know even as also I am known." In the meantime God is present and approachable through Christ and the means of grace. But even this presence implies no denouement of his majesty. The presence of Christ in worship remains a mystery, for here it is the majesty of God which is being revealed. Through the presence of Christ in worship, God makes it known that he the Omnipresent is "present-for-man" in worship. But to effect this presence is not in man's power, neither by means of "transsubstantiation" nor through a mental effort, for the presence of God in Christ is a revelation of the works of the divine Majesty.[21]

The Presence of Christ in the Lord's Supper

The presence of Christ in worship is, as shown above, a presence in the Word. The Word is that of oral preaching, for though present everywhere, Christ is comprehended in his Word.[22]

The Word is the essence of his presence, for through the Word proclaimed, all the works of God are revealed. And through the Word Christ comprehends himself in the sacraments.[23] He is here, according to his promises, "Lo, I am with you always" (Matt. 28:20), and "Where two or three are gathered in my name, there am I in the midst of them" (Matt. 18:20).

[19] *WA* 18, 709, 753. [20] *WA* 18, 684. [21] *WA* 23, 147.

[22] *WA* 17 II, 24, 132; 19, 489.

[23] *WA* 19, 493: "He revealed himself in the Word and through the Word he also comprehends himself in the bread." Cf. 47, 303.

Wherever the members of his body meet in prayer and worship, he is there.[24]

Since Christ's presence in the Word is the place of his "presence-for-us," worship may be defined as his presence in Word and sacrament within the communion of saints. His presence is related to his people and cannot be divorced from them. It cannot be considered "by itself." The Word and the sacraments are for the benefit of men, not in the sense that they concern mankind by virtue of their objective value, but only in the sense that as realities they bear a personal reference.

It was in connection with the controversies on the Lord's Supper that the problem of the presence of Christ presented itself to Luther. As we review his arguments in these controversies, we hope to clarify further the mode and meaning of the presence of Christ.[25]

In the Lord's Supper Christ is present "under the bread and wine." [26] This phrase circumscribes the "real presence."[27] Earthly means become the vehicles by which the body and blood are distributed throughout the earth. These are two characteristics of the presence of Christ: 1) It is realized in the visible, earthly means of creation and 2) under these means God reveals himself in a hidden manner. The physical nature of these vehicles of

[24] *WA* 49, 594.

[25] The doctrine of the Lord's Supper has been treated extensively in the literature on Luther. These are among the most important contributions: Karl Barth, *Ansatz und Absicht in Luthers Abendmahlslehre* (Muenchen: 1928); P.W. Gennrich, *op. cit.;* Ernst Sommerlath, *Der Sinn des Abendmahls nach Luthers Gedanken ueber das Abendmahl, 1527* (Leipzig: 1930); Helmut Gollwitzer, *Coena Domini* (Muenchen: 1937); and the symposia *Abendmahlsgemeinschaft?* ed. by H. Asmussen (Muenchen: 1938) and *Vom Sakrament des Altars,* ed. by Herman Sasse (Leipzig: 1941).

[26] *WA* 30 I, 223, 388.

[27] The "real" presence of Christ is to be distinguished from the "local" and the "speculative" presence. These last two are characteristic of the theologies of the papists and the Enthusiasts respectively.

Christ's presence is an offense to sinful man. He is prone to misunderstand the revelation of God as though it could be mastered and comprehended. But it is open only to humble faith, for the presence of Christ is hidden.[28] The Word alone reveals it. And this Word must be received in faith.[29] Thus the visible, earthly means are closely bound to the Word (as an interpretation of the sacrament) and to faith. Christ's presence is presence for the sake of our faith. God deals with us through earthly means to which he adds his Word. It is faith alone which combines the two and enables the Word of promise to make the earthly gifts a blessing for man.[30]

Roman theology applied the idea of *opus operatum* (cf. above p. 45ff) to the Sacrament and this affected their understanding of the presence of Christ. The sacraments were defined as "effectual signs" *(signa efficacia)*, because a certain rite by its mere performance *(opus operatum)* was supposed to effect the presence of Christ. Thus the benefits of Christ's presence were divorced from faith. The sacraments were thought to impart a blessing, irrespective of the faith of the recipient. They did not even need to be distributed to the congregation.

This whole idea is diametrically opposed to the theology of Luther, for he taught Christ as the One "present for us," to be received in faith. To be sure, his presence does not depend on the faith of man.[31] But one cannot count on it without by faith or

[28] *WA* 18, 212: "We teach that the body and blood are not visibly in outward things, but are concealed under the Sacrament." Cf. 51, 286.

[29] *WA* 26, 478: "Of course it is a miracle that Christ's body and blood should be in the Sacrament; nor are they visible. But we are content to know through the Word and by faith that they are there." See Luther in opposition to Karlstadt in 18, 207.

[30] *WA* 6, 363.

[31] Herbert Olsson, "The Church's Visibility and Invisibility According to Luther," in Anders Nygren (ed.), *This Is the Church* (Philadelphia: Muhlenberg, 1952), p. 226ff.

unbelief taking a stand for or against receiving the grace of God. The Sacrament must be understood as act of God received by man in the passivity of faith (cf. above p. 45).[32] Such a reception of the Sacrament implies a recognition of the sovereign will of God who uses earthly means to convey his heavenly gifts.

"There stands the Word, and it says clearly and lucidly that Christ gives his body to be eaten when he gives the bread. On this we stand, believe, and teach that truly and bodily the body of Christ is received and eaten in the Supper. But how this is effected, or in what manner he is in the bread, we do not know and are not supposed to know. We are to trust God's Word and not to limit him. Bread it is that we see with our eyes. But with our ears we hear that the body is there."[33] By accepting the Word, the believer understands the sign as God has given it: as a salutary gift (gospel) under earthly forms. Faith waits for the Holy Spirit who, though not depending on outward means, is granted through them when and where it pleases God *(ubi et quando visum est Deo)*.[34]

The real presence was also taught by the representatives of scholasticism, and Luther freely acknowledged the zeal of his opponents at this point. But he rejected their attempt to explain the real presence by the doctrine of transsubstantiation. "For the bodily indwelling of the divine nature, the human nature need not be transsubstantiated so that the divinity remains under the accidents of the humanity. Both natures remain complete and we can say: Here man is God and there God is man. Though philosophy does not grasp it, faith will."[35]

[32] *WA* 2, 751, 715. [33] *WA* 23, 87.
[34] R. Prenter, *op. cit.*, p. 292f.
[35] *WA* 6, 511. Cf. G. Ljunggren, "Luthers nattwardslaera," in *Ordet och tron* (Stockholm: 1931), p. 198. Gennrich (*op. cit.*, p. 4), emphasizes that Luther's Christology was not developed during the controversy on the Lord's

In the doctrine of transsubstantiation he detected the influence of philosophy. The scholastics had introduced the substance idea of Aristotle in order to explain the real presence. From these premises they had concluded that the Sacrament contains the substance of the body of Christ. The substance of the bread had changed, or rather been made to disappear, so that of the elements the accidents alone were left.

Luther rejected this doctrine, not as too irrational, but as too rational. Reason is bound to misinterpret the real presence. A deeper understanding of Christology made transsubstantiation pointless to him. For in Christ he found both human and divine nature to be present, without change and without mixture. Human nature therefore needs no transsubstantiation for the divine to dwell in it.[36] Faith can see both natures in one. Reason alone remains baffled. But in matters of revelation it has no voice. The real presence does not depend on transsubstantiation. "For the true body and blood to be in the Sacrament it is not necessary for the bread and wine to be transsubstantiated. Though both remain at the same time it can truly be said: 'This bread is my body, this wine is my blood' and vice versa."[37]

Natural bread and wine are the vehicles of the presence of Christ. This conviction was strengthened by Luther's understanding of the First Article of the Apostles' Creed.[38] In dealing with man God uses his own creation. The argument that created things

Supper, but that in that controversy Luther applied insights that he had formed much earlier. For the connection between Christology and the Eucharist compare Helmut Gollwitzer, "Luthers Abendmahlslehre," in *Abendmahlsgemeinschaft?* p. 100f.

[36] *WA* 6, 511.

[37] *WA* 6, 511. Cf. 18, 186. [Two pages of the original are omitted here. In them Dr. Vajta examines a number of passages interpreted in support of transsubstantiation, and refutes this interpretation. Trans.]

[38] *WA* 10 II, 208.

ought to give way to Christ is an insult to the good gifts of God, for sin is not in the created things themselves but in their abuse by sinful man.[39]

Christ's omnipresence, a direct expression of Luther's faith in the Creator, is the crowning argument against transsubstantiation.[40] Christ is in the elements long before they are placed on the altar. The eyes of sinful man cannot see him there. But faith accepts the Word which reveals his presence for the forgiveness of sins.

In contrast to the scholastic term "transsubstantiation," Luther's idea has sometimes been dubbed "consubstantiation."[41] But is it proper to employ the term "substance" at all in reference to Luther? To be sure, certain statements of the Reformer are cited in support of this interpretation.[42] But there is need for caution here. Consubstantiation suggests the philosophical approach which Luther rejected so violently. If it is used, it must be related to his idea of omnipresence, his faith in the Creator.[43]

This faith forbids the interpretation of "consubstantiation" as a temporary union of two substances. The teaching of omnipresence precludes a philosophical solution like this. The real presence cannot be analyzed by man-made formulas. It can only be illustrated by the two natures of Christ. Faith receives Christ in the Word which proclaims his presence, under the forms of

[39] *WA* 10 II, 207f. Cf. 11, 441. [40] *WA* 23, 145.

[41] It was used by Reinhold Seeberg in *Die Lehre Luthers*, p. 325; Gollwitzer, *Coena Domini*, p. 39f, 48; and Brilioth, *op. cit.*, p. 100f, 87. The term "consubstantiation" occurs nowhere in Luther. There is no reason for using this term for the "abolition of the magical" in the mass and for the "emphasis on the substantial presence of Christ," for the real presence has nothing to do with substance in the connotation of Aristotle and the scholastics.

[42] Compare especially *WA* 6, 510; 10 II, 207 (the example of the red-hot iron).

[43] For Luther's use of the idea of "substance," which for him had a meaning different from that of the Middle Ages, see Gennrich, *op. cit.*, p. 64ff.

the bread and wine, without demanding an explanation of the mode of his presence.[44] For the real presence rests on God's presence in all his works. This presence is invisible to man except by faith. God remains hidden even in his revelation. In the last analysis, faith is unconcerned about the relation of "sign" and Christ. It is content with what the Word says. Luther regretted the interest which under the impact of scholasticism had been focused on this question.[45] To him the decisive question was not the "how," but the "why" of the real presence, and he found the answer in the "for-us," that is, "for our salvation."

By the teaching of transsubstantiation Christ had been localized in the host. "The church" could dispose of his presence. The substance of the bread disappeared through consecration and under its accidents the substance of Christ's body could be seen. The invisible had been made visible, the spiritual material, the earthly divine. At the altar, the priest held Christ in his own hand. No longer could Christ dispose of his own presence. No more did the Word determine the meaning of the Supper. The church had replaced Christ as a mediator between God and man. Christ had become a tool to use and control. Redemption lay not with him, but with the church that had him in her hand and could reconcile God by the sacrifice of the mass. The real presence had become a sort of law, a human way to God, and was no longer part of the gospel through which God omnipresent and omnipotent reveals himself.[46]

Few changes were needed to turn Luther's arguments against

[44] *WA* 26, 344. In as early a work as *De captivitate* (*WA* 6, 551f) Luther had claimed that the Sacrament is a mystery.

[45] *WA* 2, 749; 6, 530; 8, 445; 6, 511.

[46] Compare R. Bring, *Kristendomstolkningar i gammal och ny tid* (Stockholm: 1950), p. 294ff, where the connection between the scholastic concern for palpability (*påtaglighet*), the concept of merit, and the neglect (*Wegdenken*) of the real presence is shown.

the scholastics also against the Enthusiasts. They too allowed philosophical concepts to color their thinking. Their objection to the real presence rested on a substantial interpretation of it. They too sought to localize Christ, not in the elements, but in a spatial heaven. "Christ is supposed to be kept in heaven as in a dungeon and stocks. It would be too ignominious for him to be with us on earth in our manifold needs of sin and death. Much better that he leave us to the devil here below and play with the angels above."[47]

Nor could they see the relation between the earthly elements and Christ glorified. In spite of their rejection of transsubstantiation, they used the same categories as the scholastics. Again it was their picture of creation—or rather the lack of it—that prevented them from accepting the presence of Christ in the elements. Theirs was a deistic notion of a god enthroned in lonely majesty, far removed from his creation. This unbiblical idea perverted their Christology. To Luther the real presence was a corollary of the incarnation. The incarnation was the real offense, and Christ's presence in worship is no more than a consequence and extension of the revelation of the omnipresent God.[48] But the deism of the Enthusiasts allowed no other presence of Christ than the mental process of remembering him.

Luther contrariwise places the "remembrance" in the Word which proclaims and offers the presence of Christ.[49] In the Supper, Christ himself is present and coming to man. There is

[47] *WA* 26, 437.

[48] *WA* 19, 500.

[49] *WA* 18, 197: "By the word 'this do in remembrance of me' (Luke 22:19) Christ means the same as St. Paul with his 'ye do show the Lord's death' (I Cor. 11:26), i.e. Christ wants us to preach about him when we receive the Sacrament, and to proclaim the gospel for the strengthening of faith. But he does not want us to sit, toy with the thoughts of our heart, and make this remembrance a good work, as dreams Dr. Carlstadt." Cf. 18, 203 and for greater detail the previous sections: *Beneficium* and *Sacrificium,* and The Proclamation of the Word, pp. 27 and 67.

no need for the flight of religious fancy by which man would leap the alleged gap between earth and heaven.[50] The "remembrance" of the Enthusiasts was a form of speculation on the divine majesty, not a believing acceptance of the real presence.[51] The same approach which had led the scholastics to the theory of transsubstantiation prompted the Enthusiasts to divorce the "sign" from the presence of Christ.[52] In either case the real presence depended on the work of man: on the one side the manipulations of the priest, and on the other the contortions of a pious soul. Both ways made the Sacrament a *Werkgeschaeft* (work business) rather than *Glaubensgeschaeft* (faith business).[53]

The Consecration as the Pledge of the Presence of Christ through the Word

For Luther, God (and Christ) is always near because of his omnipresence. This fact is expressive of God's omnipotent dominion over his creation. But Christ's "presence for us," the

[50] *WA* 33, 224ff; R. Bring, *Kristendomstolkningar*, p. 276, 298f.

[51] *WA* 40 I, 456.

[52] Luther too employs the term "symbol," but he differentiates between its theological and its philosophical meaning (see *WA* TR 4, 666). The term "sign" also belongs to the customary terminology of Luther, especially during the early years (previous to the controversies with the Enthusiasts), as E. Sommerlath (*op. cit.*, p. 102ff) emphasizes. But it must be emphasized that the application of the terms "symbol" or "sign" to the elements does not preclude the real presence. Cf. Gennrich, *op. cit.*, p. 148ff. Karl Barth's criticism of Luther's teaching on the Lord's Supper proceeds from a philosophical concept of the "symbol" which is supposed to point beyond the elements to the glorified Christ (*Christus der Herrlichkeit*) in heaven. From this viewpoint Luther is seen as too closely linked with Rome. Barth thinks that Rome as well as Luther confuse the "sign" (that which signifies) with the "signed" (that which is signified). But Barth's approach obscures the fact that the connection between Christ and the Sacrament which Luther posits is radically different from the one in the Roman church. Actually Barth is closer to Rome than Luther; for with Rome he denudes the creation of the real presence of Christ. See Karl Barth, *Ansatz und Absicht in Luthers Abendmahlslehre*, p. 59f and "Die Lehre von den Sakramenten" in *Zwischen den Zeiten* (Muenchen: 1929), p. 456f. For criticism of Barth's view see B. E. Benktson, *op. cit.*, p. 201ff.

[53] *WA* 11, 448f.

presence in which he wants to be sought and to be found, is a presence in the Word which connects the outward signs (*signa, res externae*) of creation with faith. What is needed is a revelation of the presence of God through the Holy Spirit.[54] This takes place in the church service. Here the Word of God occupies a central position, especially in connection with the distribution of the Sacrament. For the presence of the body and blood of Christ is effected by virtue of the Word (*ex virtute verbi*).[55]

Luther understood the Words of Institution as the pledge (*Verheissung, Zusagung*)[56] by which Christ has promised to be present whenever bread and wine are being administered in his name. The celebration of the Eucharist rests on our faith in these words, for it joins them to the elements through which Christ wants to be "present for us." This is the liturgical act of consecration, the significance of which we must now define.[57]

God acts in the Sacrament. His Word, his institution and command are primary in the Sacrament.[58] Man's activity has no place in it. What is being distributed is God's gift for his people. There is no room for the underlying premise of the Roman consecration—the power to sacrifice (*potestas sacrificandi*)—for this premise assumed for the clergy a power superior to that of God. The teaching of transsubstantiation was another evidence of this arrogated power, for the clergy alone was deemed able to effect it.

[54] *WA* 26, 506. [55] *WA* 6, 510.

[56] This understanding is decisive in *Sermon von dem neuen Testament* (1520) and *De abroganda missa privata* (1521). See 6, 356ff and 8, 436f.

[57] In the following we retain the term "consecration," but use it in the meaning which Luther attributed to the respective liturgical act, as distinguished from the Roman idea of consecration. In this way our use of the term is not affected by the objections of P. Althaus against it (*Die christliche Wahrheit* [Guetersloh: 1948], II, p. 397ff), though a certain vacillation in Luther's use of the term must be admitted.

[58] *WA* 30 I, 223.

Luther based the real presence on the Word. It is the promise of Christ by which he offers his gifts under bread and wine, for the Word alone has the power of granting heavenly gifts in earthly forms. In this connection Luther referred to Augustine's *Accedat verbum ad elementum et fit sacramentum* (When the word accedes to the element, it becomes a sacrament). There can be no sacrament apart from the Word.[59] Consecration is the liturgical act in which the omnipresent body and blood of Christ are revealed and promised to man, as the Word accedes to the elements, in accordance with Christ's institution and command, that they might be received by the church as God's gift for the remission of sins.

"That bread and wine should be the body and blood of Jesus is not due to our doing, speaking, or acting, let alone to our consecration [as priests], but to Christ's order, command, and institution. . . . It must be his body and blood when we meet and say his words over the bread and wine. We do no more than administer the bread and wine with his words according to his command and institution."[60]

Through the Words of Institution, God's creative Word becomes effective.[61] And with divine power, the promise of the Upper Room effects Christ's "presence for us,"[62] for the words

[59] *WA* 30^{I}, 223.

[60] *WA* 38, 240, 248. Besides *WA* 23, 147, see also 26, 287: "We do not say that the bread becomes his body, but that the body, which was made long ago, is present when we say, 'This is my body.' Christ did not command us to say: 'This is to become my body,' or 'Make this my body,' but 'This is my body.' "

[61] E. Sommerlath, *Der Sinn des Abendmahls,* p. 111f.

[62] Luther is rather inconsistent in his use of the term "consecration." In *De abroganda* (1521) he speaks as well of the words of consecration as of the words of the testament *(verba testamenti)* (*WA* 8, 433, 444, 445), but with stronger emphasis on the latter, because of his interpretation of the mass as testament. In the same work, he says about the connection of these words with the elements: "With the Word which he speaks, he makes of it his body and

"This is my body" are *Taetelworte* (action words) which create that of which they speak.[63] Thus to Luther, the consecration is nothing else but the promise of Christ's "presence for us" in the Word.

The gift of forgiveness promised in the Word is present in the elements. The word "is" is basic to Luther's defense of the real presence. The union of earthly and heavenly things in the Sacrament is a corollary of the union of divinity and humanity in the person of Christ. The sacramental union reflects the personal union on the level of the church.

Luther was greatly concerned that the consecration should not be separated from the communion. Christ effects his presence in order to be received. It is an insult to him when men worship the host instead of eating it in faith. The Roman concept of consecration made communion proper irrelevant. Nor did the Enthusiasts consider eating and drinking essential to the real presence, for to them the presence had nothing to do with the elements. Luther was of a different mind. To him, eating and drinking were constitutive parts of the presence of Christ, for God gives his gifts to be received by men.[64]

Luther's teaching should not be interpreted to mean that for-

blood and gives it to his disciples to eat" (8, 509. Cf. 513). "The sacrament is being made, blessed, and sanctified through the Word of God" (10 II, 19). In the *Formula Missae,* he speaks of *benedictio* (12, 211, 212, 214), in the *Deutsche Messe* (1526) of *Ampt oder Dermunge* (19, 97), but also of "consecration" (19, 99). The ministry has the right to "consecrate or administer the sacred bread and wine" (12, 182). In *Von der Winkelmesse* (1533) we read "consecrated or (as it is called) changed" (38, 210), *vermag und schafft* (effects and does) (240), "changes or gives" (248).

[63] *WA* 26, 282.

[64] Compare notes 57, 60 and 62 above. The texts which were quoted there show the close connection between consecration and communion. This emphasis explains two features in his liturgical formulas, namely: (1) the provision for the bread to be administered immediately after the words on them (*WA* 12, 214 and 19, 99). Knolle is quite right when he maintains that consecration and communion formed *one* liturgical act for Luther, and when he explains

giveness is by the Word alone while the elements offered food for the body.[65] Of course it is true that the Word imparts the forgiveness of sins. Christ is also present in the Word, though in a different, a bodily manner.[66] Luther stressed Christ's presence in the Word in his controversies with the Enthusiasts. He pointed out that even should it be granted that the elements are mere "signs," yet it would not be necessary for the believer to transport himself mentally to the cross of Calvary, for Christ is present here and now in his Word. "Though there should be only bread and wine, as they allege, yet as long as the words remain: 'Take and eat, this is my body, given for you,' remission of sins is offered in the Sacrament for the sake of these words."[67]

But actually, the elements are more than "signs," more than food for the body. They are the vehicles of the presence of Christ, the same presence which, in a different way, comes through the Word. As a matter of fact, it is the Word which attests to Christ's presence in the elements.[68] To divorce the presence from the elements is contrary to Luther's intention.[69]

Luther's radical reorganization of the Canon from his intention to join the consecration and communion as closely as possible. (2) the use of the Lucan and Pauline version of the Words of Institution, where after the words "this is my body" the words "which is given for you," which do not appear in Matthew and Mark, are inserted. These features stress in word and act the "for us" character of the consecration.

[65] In counteraction to this misunderstanding see *WA* 23, 181 and 189. Also H. Gollwitzer, *Luthers Abendmahlslehre*, p. 115f: "The sovereignty of the Word does not cancel the means which the Word employs. Everything comes through the Word; but the Word is not the only thing that exists. If the general proposition that God only acts through the Word should be used to deny the presence in the Sacrament of the body of Christ, the incarnation, and even the creation would be denied."

[66] Decisive for Luther were the words from Col. 2:9: "In him the whole fulness of deity dwells bodily."

[67] *WA* 18, 204.

[68] E. Sommerlath, *Der Sinn des Abendmahls*, p. 41f.

[69] The attempt to locate the real presence in the action (e.g. in Carl Stange, "Die Lehre von den Sakramenten," in *Studien des apologetischen Seminars in Wernigerode* [Guetersloh: 1920], p. 57f, and G. Ljunggren, *Synd och Skuld,*

As shown above, Luther based the sacramental union on the Words of Institution. These words, read in the service, reveal the presence of Christ, not by offering information on a purely intellectual level, but by proclaiming the redemptive activity of Christ. It was as important for Luther to maintain (against Rome) that natural bread and wine are the vehicles of the real presence as to stress (against the Enthusiasts) that the elements are no longer "mere bread and wine" after the Words of Institution have been spoken over them. "As we say of baptism that it is not simply water, so also we say here that the Sacrament is bread and wine, not simply bread and wine as is otherwise put on the table, but bread and wine comprehended in God's Word and united with it. It is the Word, I say, that makes the Sacrament and the distinction so that it is not simply bread and wine, but the body and blood of Christ."[70]

To be sure, they have not been changed "in substance." But they have been set apart from every other created thing. While other things of this world serve our present life, the consecrated elements have been placed in the service of the new creation, the body and blood of the crucified Saviour. "Our only concern is whether the promise and command are present, for by these,

pp. 198f, 211) must therefore be considered a psychologizing of Luther's view of the things of creation. This thought comes from Schleiermacher. A representative act seems more easily comprehensible than the presence of Christ as real gift in the elements. See Sommerlath, *Der Sinn des Abendmahls*, p. 19. If the bodily presence of Christ in bread and wine is denied, it is necessary to explain Luther's references to bodily blessings of the Supper as unevangelical influences from the church fathers. (See Ljunggren, *Synd och Skuld.*) For a critique of this view see Prenter, *op. cit.*, p. 274ff, where he shows that the bodily presence of Christ and bodily blessings from the Supper belong together and have nothing to do with nature mysticism. A tendency toward the above-mentioned dissolution of the real presence can also be seen in Paul Althaus' definition of the Sacrament as *Tatgleichnis* (acted-out parable). Gollwitzer's criticism is well taken when he says (*Coena Domini*, p. 34): "Whoever proceeds from the action stands thereby outside of the proper Lutheran doctrine of the Lord's Supper. That is true from Melanchthon to Althaus."

[70] *WA* 30 I, 223. Cf. 25, 384.

the creatures are vested with a new power beyond the power which they have by nature."[71] This function is unique. Other earthly gifts do not share it, not even bread and wine in ordinary use. It takes the promise of Christ and receptive faith. Without these Christ, though present everywhere, cannot be found.[72]

This point again reflects the twofold manner of Christ's presence which we discussed earlier. The Enthusiasts viewed the Supper as an ordinary meal, while Luther insisted on its uniqueness with Christ at hand as both the Giver and the Gift,[73] for if the Eucharist were no more than any other supper, the Christian's every meal would become a sacrament. This is not so. Through the Word alone the Supper becomes a gift of salvation, and the food that is eaten becomes more than bread and wine.

That is not to say that "mere bread and wine" have no relation to the Word. The Word points to Him who grants these gifts and to our duty to receive the same with thanks.[74] But he who eats his daily bread with thanks does not thereby receive a sacrament. A table prayer, though it be pronounced by Christ himself, does not make bread and wine into the Supper of the Lord. "For we know that ordinary bread remains the same and does not become a heavenly gift, though Christ and all the apostles should bless it. Christ in John 6 divided the bread

[71] *WA* 42, 171. The problem of the duration of the presence of Christ in the Sacrament was for Luther a marginal question which he hardly touched upon. His concept of omnipresence protected him from such speculations. Christ is present when the elements are put to use (*in Gebrauch genommen*) through the consecration. But the ideas of *usus* (use) and *sumptio* (eating and drinking) are not congruent to Luther. With the consecration, the *usus* has begun, and the gifts are offered for the *sumptio*. But if the *sumptio* is omitted, the *usus sacramenti* ceases too, and that disposes of the question of Christ's continued presence. Luther's practice with regard to leftover elements need not be interpreted as a carryover from the Roman view of consecration.

[72] *WA* 23, 151.

[73] *WA* 23, 271, 149.

[74] Compare the interpretation of the Fourth Petition in *WA* 30 I, 373.

among the people and thanked and praised God for it, yet it remained ordinary bread and did not become heavenly bread."[75]

The gifts of the Redeemer call forth a response different from the response to those of the Creator. The Creator requires man to distinguish that which is made from the one who made it.[76] But in the Redeemer he must acknowledge the union of the two natures, human and divine.[77] This distinction reflects the two modes of God's presence in creation and in the incarnation (and in the church).

Thus Christ's presence in the Word and Sacrament must be viewed under the aspect of sacramental union. A christological parallel may serve to illustrate this fact. Faith sees in every man a creature of the Lord. To kill a man means to kill one who was created by God. But to kill the Son is to kill God himself. "In Christ is something other, higher, and greater than in all other creatures, for in him God is not simply present as in all others. God dwells in him bodily so that man and God are one person. And though I can say of all creatures, 'God is there or in them,' I cannot say, 'This is God himself.' But of Christ faith confesses not only that God is in him, but: 'This is God himself.' "[78]

The same is true of bread and wine. In one respect they are earthly gifts, given by God for food and drink. In another, they are heavenly gifts, administered in the Eucharist. It is true that on the altar as well as on the table, they remain true bread and wine. Yet with the Word, they are more than mere bread and wine; they are the body and blood of Christ, given and offered for us. In opposing the Enthusiasts, Luther gave greater emphasis to the fact that the elements are "not mere bread and

[75] *WA* 23, 231.

[76] *WA* 40 I, 174.

[77] Compare Luther's rejection of the idea of *alloiosis* (26, 319) and his defense of the *communicatio idiomatum*. Cf. *WA* 26, 443.

[78] *WA* 23, 141.

wine" than to the complementary truth that they are "ordinary" earthly gifts.[79] But in order to maintain fully the real presence of Christ, both definitions are necessary.[80]

The consecration as Luther understood it is based on the difference between God's work in creation and in redemption (in the church). It implies no separation of the holy from the profane, for God fills all of creation. But it reveals the Redeemer's dominion over creation. Christ redeems creation by gathering his elect from the common stock of humanity. But his presence is bound to the Word and the sacraments, and as the latter belong to the created world they are apt to be abused, as are all the things of this world. They cannot be rightly used without faith. Christ will be known only by those who receive the Word and sacraments in faith. Such men will find all of creation to be filled with the presence of God and Christ. They use creatures of the world in faith as members of the church which is creation restored.

Luther's explanation of the First Article may therefore well be called the creed of the Christian,[81] for Christ opened no special spiritual province to the believer. Luther even referred to the creature as a vehicle of the forgiveness of sins.[82] But this must be understood in line with the words "without any merit or worthiness in me," that is, of God's spontaneous and unmotivated love which can also be seen in his temporal gifts. He showers his gifts on the evil as on the good.[83] But this fact does not erase

[79] *WA* 26, 462: "Before I would, with the Enthusiasts, accept mere wine, I would rather with the pope accept mere blood." Compare also the whole paragraph culminating in the realistic statement: "Thus the wine in the Lord's Supper is no longer a fruit of the vine; for the latter is surely nothing but mere ordinary wine."

[80] *WA* 26, 443. [81] *WA* 30 I, 362ff. [82] *WA* TR 1, 815.

[83] Cf. A. Nygren, *Agape and Eros* (Philadelphia: Westminster, 1953), p. 731ff and the passages quoted there.

the difference between the gifts of God by which he preserves our earthly life and those by which he grants life eternal. Otherwise the christological aspect of creation, which is so essential for linking creation and redemption, would be lost.[84] And the discussion would veer around to the possibilities of free will—natural man's attempt to meet God and gain salvation apart from the means of grace.

The spiritual presence of Christ reveals the world of creation as the place of the natural presence of God. The Word (with the sacraments) is the window through which we see God as the One who redeems us in and for creation.[85] Christ's work implies no separation of creation and redemption. He made certain created things his tools, because he reserved the work of redemption for himself. Thus he lays bare the sin which perverts man's relation to the Creator and his creatures. But through his presence in creation, he also opens for believers an entrance to God.

[84] Cf. H. Lilje, *Luthers Geschichtsauffassung* (Zuerich: 1932), especially p. 86ff. Torgny Bohlin, in his study *Den korsfaeste Skaparen* (Stockholm: 1952), has shown that in Luther, creation must be understood from the soteriological viewpoint, that is, from God's work in Christ. See especially Chapter 1.

[85] *WA* 31 II, 655.

5

The Office of the Ministry as Impartation of the Gift of God

Worship, as we have concluded, is God's work of love by which he imparts to us the fruits of the redemption in Jesus Christ. This work is done through the Word and the sacraments. But we also found that the Word must be preached and the sacraments administered. It is not enough for the Word to rest between the covers of the Bible, nor for the Sacrament to be displayed in the tabernacle on the altar. The Word is a message. It must be heard.[1] It needs messengers. The Sacrament is a gift. It must be received. It requires administrators.

The Ministry as a Service for Others

So we must consider the office of the ministry. To Luther, worship and the ministry were intimately connected, for worship is nothing but the office through which Christ is present in and with his gifts of grace. This implies the important conclusion that the office receives its validity from the Word and the sacraments. It is a handmaid of the Word, a ministry—a service—of the Word of God (*ministerium verbi divini*).[2]

This dependence cannot be reversed. The Word and the sacraments need no authorization on the part of the ecclesiastical office.[3] With this assertion Luther stood against Rome. For in

[1] *WA* 10 I, 1, 329; 11, 411; 12, 191. [2] *WA* 6, 566; 8, 422; 2, 180.
[3] *WA* 39 II, 182: "The ministry of the Word makes ministers, not the ministers the ministry." Cf. 38, 238. Whenever Luther enumerates the marks

the Roman church, the handmaid had become the mistress, as the hierarchy assumed authority to decide what is the Word of God and claimed the power to effect transsubstantiation and so to "make" the Sacrament. Far from serving the work of Christ, the priesthood had arrogated to itself jurisdiction over the means of grace.[4]

This development had brought on one further consequence. The accent had moved from the office as an institution of God to the officiant as a person of authority. From a function, the ministry had become a rank. And the fiction of "apostolic succession" was needed in order to guarantee the legitimacy of the ministry and therewith indirectly of the means of grace.[5] This fiction is incompatible with the Lutheran idea of the office. The Christian ministry receives its proper authorization not from an ecclesiastical pedigree but from the Word and the sacraments.

As a function the ministry can never be an end in itself. Its one and only purpose is to serve others. Luther's view of the ministry is inseparable from his picture of worship as a benefit granted to us by God.[6] But in order to understand its place in the whole of Luther's theology we must see the ministry in the context of his teaching on the two kingdoms. God imparts his benefits to mankind through two kingdoms. In the temporal kingdom he grants earthly gifts (including civil righteousness),

of the church, he names first the Word and the sacraments, then the office which imparts these gifts. Cf. 50, 632.

[4] *WA* 38, 253.

[5] *WA* 39 II, 176ff. For Luther's view of the apostolic succession see R. Askmark, *Aembetet i den svenska kyrkan* (Lund: 1949), p. 310ff and H. H. Kramm, *The Theology of Martin Luther* (London: 1947), p. 70ff and 74ff. Cf. also 49, 139; 38, 240.

[6] G. Hoek, "Luthers laera om kyrkans aembete," in *En bok om kyrkans aembete* (Stockholm: 1951); English trans. in *Scottish Journal of Theology* I (1954), p. 16ff; Conrad Bergendoff, *The Revelation and the Ministry of Grace* (Stockholm: 1950); R. Josefson, "Det andlige aembetet i Svenska kyrkans bekaennelseskrifter," in *En bok om kyrkans aembete.*

in the spiritual kingdom eternal life (and therewith the righteousness of faith). In these two kingdoms God acts through different offices: secular authority, the family, and the holy ministry.[7] The offices, though different in function, are all of equal rank.[8] Through the secular estates God cares for the temporal well-being of men, through the ministry for their eternal good. Both offices have divine sanction. But neither gives its incumbents special claims or status before God. The office may be holy and divine, but not necessarily so the office bearer.[9] The latter has only the call to set him apart from the rank and file of his fellow-Christians. And one must clearly distinguish between what a man is and does as a private individual and what he is and does as a father, ruler, pastor, etc. There is absolutely no basis for the division of Christendom into clergy and laity as two classes different in rank and sanctity. This invention of the Roman church is a sectarian assault on the unity of the church,[10] and exalts man-made methods of salvation at the expense of God's own creation.[11]

But while a minister may be not a whit holier or better than a soldier or a hangman, his office is incomparably higher, for the kind of authority the ministry possesses is far different from that which secular estates enjoy. The latter have authority *delegated by God.* The prince, for example, has real power within the secular realm over his subjects. But spiritual authority is of a different kind. It is authority reserved for God. Properly speak-

[7] The teaching of the two kingdoms has been extensively treated. Cf. G. Wingren, *Luther on Vocation,* pp. 1-77.

[8] *WA* 8, 429; 6, 408; 31 I, 217; Werner Elert, *Morphologie des Luthertums* (Muenchen: 1931), I, p. 304.

[9] *WA* 6, 380; 10 I, 1, 496; 6, 541.

[10] *WA* 6, 407; 12, 130; 8, 429; 6, 563; 8, 430.

[11] *WA* 8, 433; 6, 566; 30 II, 500.

ing, Christ is the sole head of the church and the only one who has authority. By arrogating to himself this position, the pope made himself the Antichrist.[12]

As a matter of fact, the ministry is Christ's continued activity on earth. In the pulpit he speaks through the mouth of the preacher,[13] at the font he himself is the Baptist,[14] at the altar he imparts the remission of sins through the hands of the minister.[15] There is no delegation of authority here. The minister is simply an instrument of the Holy Spirit, and his office a kind of stewardship.[16] He has no authority over the Word and sacraments apart from his call to administer them to the congregation.[17] The same applies logically to the power of the keys. It rests not with the pope, but with Christ. We can do no more than declare the forgiveness which Christ obtained for us on the cross.[18] Otherwise the ministry becomes a sort of tyranny over the souls of men for whose benefit it has been instituted. For what the minister by virtue of his call receives from Christ he must pass on to his fellow-men for their eternal salvation. In so doing, he "co-operates" with God.[19] That is not to say that he

[12] For this reason it is also impossible for the church to have a visible head. Here the parallel between the church and secular government breaks down. See, for example, *WA* 6, 297ff.

[13] *WA* 20, 350; 30 [II], 498.

[14] *WA* 47, 451; 38, 239.

[15] *WA* 49, 140.

[16] *WA* 6, 564; 12, 190; 11, 271; 6, 543; 8, 428. But secular rulers, in marked contrast to the spiritual, may be called "gods," "lords," etc. (*WA* 31 [I], 191, with reference to Ps. 82:1).

[17] *WA* 6, 530. Cf. 38, 242, where Luther stresses the parallelism between God's work of creation and redemption; also 38, 240 and 239: "Our baptizing should be called an impartation or bestowal of the baptism of Christ, even as our preaching is an impartation of the Word of God." Cf. 7, 495.

[18] *WA* 1, 233, 545.

[19] *WA* 17 [II], 179; 44, 648: "Paul calls the apostles co-operators of God. Indeed, he alone operates, but he operates through us." Cf. 43, 81; also G. Wingren, *Luther on Vocation*, p. 123ff.

could add anything of his own, not even the external form.[20] Yet his office is essential, for Christ imparts the Word to men, not vertically from above (*senkrecht von oben*), but rather through the medium of human tongues and voices.

Finally, this idea of co-operation implies the possibility of abuse. The minister of Christ may fail to fulfil his appointed task or he may usurp the grace which he was called to impart to others. Luther noted both forms of non-co-operation. An instance of the first was the service of the mass of the Roman priests. It was no more than a caricature of the holy ministry, for the sacrifice which they presumed to bring was a fiction invented by the devil and not a function ordained of God. This office had nothing in common with the Christian ministry. The other perversion, against which Luther warned equally often, was the glorification of the ministry as a calling more divine than others. This abuse was not quite as serious as the first. Though it might corrupt the personal faith of the incumbent, it did not necessarily affect the validity of the office which he rendered, for where the means of grace are administered in accordance with Christ's institution, there is a valid ministry, irrespective of the personal faith of the pastor. The wickedness of his servants cannot hinder God from imparting his grace to his children.[21]

Ordination as the Call into the Ministry

The question has often been raised as to whether Luther's picture of the ministry should be called institutional or sociological. Is the office of the ministry a divine institution or a human appointment? The question admits of no unqualified answer for both views occur in Luther's writings.

In the last section the stress was on the institutional character

[20] *WA* 6, 530.
[21] *WA* 50, 634; 38, 240, 243; 6, 526; 26, 164.

of the ministry. It is God's institution. God acts in and through it, irrespective of the fitness of the minister. But there is also a congregational aspect to Luther's idea of the office. As is well known, he claimed the right for the congregation to call preachers who would act "on behalf of the congregation." Modern scholars have found it very difficult to reconcile the institutional and the sociological aspects in Luther's view of the ministry.[22] But the Reformer himself was unaware of these alleged contradictions. It was the idea of co-operation that solved the dilemma for him. A closer examination of Luther's view of the call may help to bring this emphasis into sharper focus.

The exigencies of the moment compelled Luther to rethink, on the basis of Scripture, the meaning of the call.[23] Traditionally, the right of ordination had rested with the bishop. Luther had no quarrel with this arrangement, but the German bishops remained solidly on the side of Rome and refused to ordain evangelical ministers. In this predicament, Luther claimed for the congregation the right of calling pastors.[24] He saw no basic difference between a call from the congregation and one from the bishop; for even the latter could function only "instead and on behalf of the congregation."[25] In other words, the congregation alone can issue a valid call, and other persons cannot exercise this right

[22] This approach to the problem came out of the theological discussion of the nineteenth century. See H. Fagerberg, *Bekenntnis, Kirche und Amt in der deutschen konfessionellen Theologie des 19. Jahrhunderts* (Uppsala: 1952); G. Rietschel, *Lehrbuch der Liturgik* II, p. 410ff and *Luther und die Ordination* (Wittenberg: 1889), p. 101f; Ruben Josefson, "The Ministry as an Office in the Church," in A. Nygren, *This Is the Church,* p. 275f, 278f.

[23] *WA* 11, 411.

[24] This he developed especially in two of his writings: *The Right and Authority of a Christian Congregation to Adjudicate Doctrines and to Call and Depose Ministers* (1523), in *WA* 11, 408-16; and *On the Institution of Ecclesiastical Offices* (1523) in *WA* 12, 169-96.

[25] *WA* 6, 407. *WA* 11, 413ff proves that the bishop may not appoint a preacher without the consent of the congregation; also 8, 253.

unless they have been delegated by the congregation.[26] For, properly speaking, all Christians are priests. It is only for the sake of love and order that an individual is singled out to exercise the functions of the ministry.[27]

"Things which we have not been commanded to do are no concern of ours. We have enough to do with the things that we have been commanded to do. It is of no avail to say, 'All Christians are priests.' Certainly all Christians are priests. But not all are pastors, for beyond the fact that a man is a Christian and a priest, he must also have an office and a parish that he has been commanded to serve. It is the call and the command which makes the pastor and preacher." [28] No one may arrogate the office to himself, because all have the same right, and it is only with their consent that a man may assume the authority of the pastorate.[29] As a matter of fact, every office needs a call, for it is the call which assures a man that he is fulfilling God's will rather than his own.

The call which the church extends is a call from God. The people through whom it comes, whether congregation or bishop, are only instruments in the hand of God, for, the apostles and prophets excepted, God calls no one directly. "The divine call is twofold, direct and indirect. . . . The apostles were called directly by God, as were the prophets in the Old Testament. But the apostles later called their own disciples; for example, Paul called Timothy, Titus, etc., and they in their turn the bishops, as Titus 1

[26] *WA* 12, 190. Cf. 12, 191, 389; 38, 230.

[27] For example, see *WA* 8, 423; 11, 413; 30 III, 524: "Much less is it to be tolerated that a sneaking outsider or layman should dare to preach in a church without a call." Cf. 32, 483; 31 I, 211: "Even in a popish congregation, a man should not preach without a proper call."

[28] *WA* 31 I, 211.

[29] *WA* 12, 189, 317; 38, 230; 6, 408. W. Elert, *Morphologie des Luthertums,* I, p. 300.

[:5]. The bishops called their own successors up to the present, and from here to the end of the world. This is an indirect call, since it comes through man, yet it is divine."[30] God always employs men as the masks (*larvae*) through which he speaks. The call to the ministry rests on the co-operation between the congregation and God. "We must believe and not doubt that God wrought and did what was done and covenanted this way by the common consent of the believers who acknowledge and confess the gospel."[31] "Christians must be sure that they are in the kingdom of God and that they do nothing, especially in spiritual matters concerning the salvation of souls, except in the certainty that not they are working, but God through them."[32]

With this view Luther stood squarely against the Enthusiasts. Where he stresses the external call, they had recourse to an inner, immediate call from the Holy Spirit. They disdained the external call as much as the external Word and the external sacraments. But Luther questioned the legitimacy of their boasted revelations and inspirations. "The parish pastor is in charge of the pulpit, baptism, and the Sacrament, and the care of all souls is committed to him. But now they want secretly to cut out the parish pastor who is in possession of the call, yet they fail to prove their secret call. They are fine thieves and murderers of souls, revilers and enemies of Christ and his church."[33]

The Holy Spirit always employs externals, and calls no man except through the congregation, for the congregation is the body of Christ and dare not shrink its responsibility of calling a pastor. Ministers do not fall from the sky, but must be chosen

[30] *WA* 40 I, 59. Cf. *WA* 16, 33.
[31] *WA* 12, 191.
[32] *WA* 17 II, 185.
[33] *WA* 30 III, 519. Cf. 30 III, 518; 31 I, 210ff.

from the ranks of the congregation with prayerful consideration and confidence in the promises of God.[34]

The divinity of the call does not preclude, but rather demands a careful examination of the candidates' qualifications.[35] Christian love and good order call for the employment of every human faculty. Nor does a majority vote impair the validity of the call.[36] As a matter of fact, such a vote has little to do with political democracy. It is simply the priesthood of believers in action.[37]

What has been said about the right of the congregation to call their pastor applies however only to normal conditions. The case is different in emergency situations where the regular procedure of calling a minister cannot be used. Here the Christian layman may exercise the function of the ministry even without a proper call, but as a priest of Christ by virtue of his baptism. "When a pastor abandons his office, he terminates his own ministry and another member of the congregation may take his place."[38] "Nor must the fact be overlooked that the office of the church is not confined to the public services in God's house. It is also exercised by the head of the family. He has the call to teach his family the Word of God. This is not a provision for emergencies; the call to teach his own is given right in and with the estate of head of the household."[39]

[34] See *WA* 11, 411; 12, 191; 38, 253, where Luther cites Matt. 18:19.

[35] See *WA* 8, 424-425. The context discusses the question why women should forego the ministry. The same question is touched upon in 50, 633 and 12, 309 where Luther adds: "But in a place where there should be no men at all, but only women as in a convent, one could also appoint a woman to preach." Cf. 30 III, 524; 1, 411.

[36] Luther points out that in the ancient church the election of popes and bishops proceeded in this manner. See *WA* 11, 415.

[37] *WA* 11, 409.

[38] *WA* 11, 412-413. See 11, 412: "The same applies in places where there are no other Christians. Here the lone Christian among unbelievers must heed the Great Commission."

[39] *WA* 12, 171; 32, 303; 30 I, 392.

Luther even maintained that the housefather is fully entitled to administer Holy Communion. But he did not mention this right among the father's duties, because he considered the Lord's Supper a public service of the congregation.[40] In emergencies he allowed every Christian to perform baptisms, women included, and he considered these emergency administrations proper functions of the office of the church.[41]

The ministry of the church is one. The occasional service of "lay" people does not establish an "emergency ministry," but proves the width and breadth of the one and only ministry, that of the Word which transcends the bounds of a static order. If necessary, Christ can found his church through the services of a single Christian who is a true priest and missionary by virtue of his baptism. Luther conceived of an episcopal church without "apostolic succession."[42]

It is not the right to minister which a pastor receives from the congregation, but only the appointment and charge. The call does not establish a special priesthood. It only indicates the particular territory where the priesthood common to all may be exercised by the designated individual.

The ministry is a public office (*ministerium publicum*). The call must therefore be made public too in order to make the incumbent known to the whole congregation. The people need to know to whom they should go to hear the Word and receive the sacraments.[43] This is the purpose of the rite of ordination. Luther saw in the ordination nothing but a public certification of the call.[44] This is why he unconditionally rejected the Roman

[40] *WA* 38, 191, 193; 39 I, 154.

[41] *WA* 12, 181.

[42] *WA* 12, 194.

[43] *WA* 38, 228.

[44] G. Rietschel, *Luther und die Ordination*, p. 49ff. P. Drews, "Vorwort zum Ordinationsformular in der Weimarer Ausgabe," *WA* 38, 401ff; and U. Altmann, "Hilfsbuch zur Geschichte des christlichen Kultus," in *Zum Kultus der Reformatoren* (Berlin: 1947), p. 65.

view of ordination. For in this view ordination had become a "consecration," a rite of anointing supposed to impart a special sanctity to the candidate. "To ordain is not to consecrate. Thus when we have a devout man, we set him aside, and by virtue of the Word which we have, we confer on him the authority of preaching the Word and administering the sacraments. This is to ordain."[45]

To the Roman church, ordination had become a sacrament. But as a sacrament, Luther pointed out, it had no legitimacy, for it carried no promise of eternal salvation as did baptism and the Lord's Supper in Christ's own words.[46] Instead it threatened to obscure the true sacraments, for it seemed to offer other and better graces than those that are every Christian's birthright by baptism. To Luther the call (*vocatio*) and ordination (*ordinatio*) were synonymous. In the laying on of hands, which the apostles and the church fathers had practiced, he saw simply a call to the ministry of the Word.[47]

It was this latter function that the Roman parish priests lacked. Their ordination entitled them to perform the sacrifice of the mass. They received the power to consecrate and sacrifice (*potestas consecrandi et sacrificandi*), as was illustrated in the presentation of the cup during the ceremony.[48] But they were not appointed to preach the Word of God.

This perversion of the ministry made Luther furious. He insisted that the church of Christ has no ministry of sacrifice. Priests who have no other function than this are not the servants of Christ. Their office is an insult to God, and their work a ministry of the devil.[49]

[45] *WA* 15, 721. Cf. 73, 459; 8, 459; 38, 195.
[46] *WA* 6, 561.
[47] *WA* 38, 228, 238, 256; H. H. Kramm, *op. cit.*, p. 81ff.
[48] *WA* 12, 173.
[49] *WA* 8, 418.

He also noted that parish priests who were appointed to preach were called by and installed in their congregations, even in the Roman church. This rite conformed to his idea of ordination, for to him, the public certification of the call (with prayer and laying on of hands) was the true ordination.[50]

From this it follows that ordination gives no personal qualification to the candidate. There is no indelible character (*character indelebilis*).[51] If a pastor, called into the ministry of the Word, fails to preach the gospel of Christ, he is no longer in the ministry, for it is not his person but the work of God that makes the ministry what it is.[52] Again, if a pastor leaves his charge, is suspended from it, or enters some other work, he reverts to the common rank and file of the church.[53] And in order to resume the ministry at a later date, he needs a new call and a new ordination.

This picture of the ministry also erased the distinction between different orders in the hierarchy. Luther knew of only one office, the ministry of the Word.[54] There was no room for the office of the presbyter (parish priest) whose only function it was to render the sacrifice of the mass. As for the deacons, Luther wanted to restore to them their original charitable tasks instead

[50] See P. Drews, *WA* 38, 408, and G. Rietschel, *Luther und die Ordination*, p. 50ff, on the religious character of the call as ordination. But we maintain in opposition to Drews that Luther did not want to abolish the public rite before the congregation with prayer and laying on of hands. Ordination was for Luther more than a juridical act. See 12, 173, 172; 38, 236, 220, 221.

[51] *WA* 6, 562, 567; 12, 190, 172; and Holl, *Gesammelte Aufsaetze*, I, p. 338.

[52] *WA* 6, 566; 15, 721.

[53] *WA* 6, 408. Hj. Lindroth in his article ("Kyrkans aembete i principiell belysning," in *En bok om kyrkans aembete*), developed the idea of the office as a representation of Christ. The danger in this lies in the fact that the accent moves from the office to the officiant and so opens the door for the idea of the indelible character. Lindroth, in spite of his strictures on Roman views (p. 282f), has not quite overcome this difficulty.

[54] R. Askmark, *op. cit.*, p. 228ff; Josefson, "The Ministry as an Office in the Church," in Nygren, *This is the Church*, p. 269ff.

of the liturgical assistance at mass that had fallen to their lot.[55] Thus, of the whole hierarchy, the episcopate alone was left. Luther took this as an office of preaching the gospel,[56] and referred proudly to his brothers in the parish ministry as bishops.[57]

The preaching of the Word is the dominant function of the ministry. This was the task to which Christ and the apostles attended.[58] With the call to preach goes therefore the call to everything that pertains to it, such as administration of the sacraments, pastoral care, etc., for the ministry rests on the proclamation of the gospel.

The Mutual Relationship of God and Faith

We have found Luther's whole approach to be based on the mutual relationship of God and faith. A consideration of worship as the work of God leads on to faith as the work of man.

So far, our consideration of worship has been somewhat incomplete for we could no more than hint at how the act of God connects with the faith of men. In the chapters that follow our discussion will focus on the role of faith in worship. Because of the "togetherness" of God and faith, we will have to refer to what has been said before on worship as the work of God, for worship, as we saw it, helps us to see the place of faith. Now we shall view the same picture from a different angle—that of faith.

We noted how Jesus Christ comes to us through worship, through both the Word and the Sacrament. Now we shall ask what he works in us by his real "presence in faith." For thus the true worship of creation, of which God had been robbed and

[55] *WA* 6, 566.

[56] *WA* 57, 171; 7, 464; 8, 429; 10 I, 2, 121; 19, 600; 10 II, 138, 143. Luther identified bishops with presbyters in 2, 387, 390.

[57] See for example *WA* 12, 205ff; 8, 429.

[58] *WA* 8, 391; 7, 50; 11, 415.

which had been restored to mankind through the faith-inspiring work of Christ, is set up again.

The picture of worship as a gift of God implies faith on the side of man and praise and thanksgiving as its expression. And as we turn to the complementary thought of worship as the work of faith, we will not be able to forget that worship is God coming to us in Christ. For only in its relation to the work of God can the work of faith be understood aright.

WORSHIP AS THE WORK OF FAITH

6

Faith and Worship

What if anything has faith to do with worship? A well-known passage in Luther's *Deutsche Messe* explains that worship should serve to inspire faith.[1] On this basis, worship has often been defined as a school of faith. For the advocates of the so-called "pedagogical" view, worship is but a means to an end. When this end has been achieved and faith has been awakened, worship has played its role. In addition, it might be used to strengthen and deepen the faith of the believers. But basically it remains an institute of the mature in faith for converting unbelievers.[2]

But this view of worship has not been uncontested. Faith is not the end but the beginning of worship. True worship is an expression of faith in prayer, praise, and thanksgiving.[3] It is the reflection of the "mood of ownership" (*Besitzerstimmung*), so characteristic of the faith of the early Christians and of Luther.[4] This idea too can boast an impressive array of Luther passages for its support.[5] We must examine Luther's understanding of faith more closely in order to resolve this dilemma between two opposing interpretations of his theology of worship.

[1] *WA* 19, 75. Cf. 2, 686.

[2] H. Jacoby, *Die Liturgik der Reformatoren* (1871-76), I, p. 155.

[3] J. Gottschick (*op. cit.*, pp. 11ff, 26ff) leans mostly on *Vermahnung zum Sakrament* (1530), and certain psalm expositions, while L. Fendt (*op. cit.*) consults mostly the *Sermon von den guten Werken* (1520), and stresses the importance of faith in contrast to works.

[4] L. Fendt, *op. cit.*, p. 194ff.

[5] See, for example, *WA* 8, 172; 10 I, 1, 675; 40 I, 360; 6, 204; 8, 10; etc.

To Believe is to Share in the Works of God

Man as a creature is bound to believe and trust. This is the law implanted in him by his Creator.[6] Faith directs man to God who thus grants him fellowship. It cannot be understood in isolation *(als etwas Fuer-sich-seiendes)* but only in relation to God.

This is true even after the fall of man. Sinful man too must believe and trust. When he thinks he is free of God, he is in fact in bond to a tyrant who claims his allegiance for himself. This is faith in reverse—unbelief. Man is so created that his existence must be marked either by faith or by unbelief, that is either by God for us in Christ, or by the devil against us.[7] It is impossible to describe faith in purely psychological categories,[8] for it is being created for a Lord and being determined by a Lord. Apart from its Lord, it does not come into focus at all. In fact, faith in God and faith in the devil are indistinguishable on the psycho-

[6] Compare above p. 4ff.

[7] The problem of faith belongs with that of Christ's indwelling by faith and therewith also with the question of conscience and of the inner man. Compare here Ragnar Bring, "Ordet, samvetet och den inre maenniskan," in *Ordet och tron.* Luther understands faith as being related to God, not as something outside of man, but as an existence determined by God, here and now. The approach which begins with certain "metaphysical" dogmas, "beyond the limits of human experience" and subsequently adds faith as an assent to these dogmas "in relation to myself," has missed Luther's idea of faith from the start. When Luther made the doctrine of justification by faith the basic condition of Christianity which creates and preserves the church (40 I, 49), he expressed exactly this idea, for the "pure doctrine" (*reine Lehre*) according to Luther is that the believer accepts the work of Christ as a reality determining his present existence, and not as an event of the past from which derive certain metaphysical dogmas and speculations which should be believed. It is only within the framework of this "pure doctrine" that the well-known differentiation of faith in knowledge, assent, and trust may be made.

[8] H. J. Iwand, *Rechtfertigungslehre und Christusglaube* (Leipzig: 1930), p. 14, writes to the point when he says: "He [Luther] did not base his explanation and definition of faith on the empirical act. He defined the empirical act on the basis of his concept of faith. Therewith he avoided the mistake that others after him were no longer able to escape—the introduction of a psychological element which was uncritically accepted into theological thought."

logical level. It is the Lord of faith who marks true from false faith. For Christ is much more than the object of our faith. He is active and present within it.

Of course his presence is neither visible nor unmediated. The end has not come. But while we wait for Christ's return, he meets us in the means of grace. This advent is invisible and indirect, requiring faith on the part of man.

Through his Holy Spirit he meets mankind as the one who is present in Word and sacrament. His presence in the church implies that it is hidden, a presence in faith. His presence is not one which we could govern or of which we could dispose, but rather one in which we may believe, that is, one by which we may be governed. Christ's presence in faith is no spiritualizing idea to Luther. For he is present in faith, not without visible means, but through them.

We stand here at the intersection of worship and faith. If to believe means to have Christ present within, then faith cannot be without worship, for the church service is the place where Christ meets man through Word and sacraments. On this redemptive work of Christ the believer rests his faith, while unbelievers bypass the activity of God and put their confidence in their own works. As fellowship between the "God-for-us" and man, faith constitutes the highest form of worship.[9]

This definition of the Christian faith shows the underlying unity between the opposing interpretations of worship quoted above. All that was needed was to interpret aright the meaning of faith. The "pedagogical" view was right in stressing the Christian faith's dependence on Word and sacrament. Faith exists only in receiving. It is not a state to enter or a character to gain. Otherwise it might become a human accomplishment to be pre-

[9] *WA* 40 I, 360.

sented to God. Luther never speaks of faith in this way except when he refers to a false, perverted faith.[10]

Faith never outgrows the "school" of worship so that worship could change to a kind of "refresher course." Faith is not a safe for storing the past mercies of God, but an open hand receiving daily the grace of God in Word and sacrament.[11] On the other hand, faith is infinitely more than worship spiritualized *("vergeistigter" Gottesdienst)*. It cannot be confined to the "inner" life of man for it depends on the "outward" means of grace. True and false worship are distinguished, not by their respective degree of "inwardness," but by their relation to the work of God.

Here the organic connection between the two sections of our study can be seen again. Faith dare not be isolated from God's redemptive action in Word and sacraments as it reaches us through the office of the ministry. God's work is the ground and cause of faith. Again it is through faith alone that worship as the work of God becomes the work of man, and therewith a fulfilment of the First Commandment. The worship which God requires of man is that which he inspires in him through Christ alone. Man becomes a "priest"[12] "passively," as it were, by re-

[10] This is the reason for his criticism of the so-called *habitus* (faith as an attitude) which plays so important a role in the Roman as well as the Enthusiast idea of faith.

[11] It is especially under the influence of R. Hermann that Luther research has stressed the fact that faith implies growth (*Fortschritt*), not however in a psychological sense (as a quantitative idea), but in reference to the ongoing work of Christ (as a temporal view). Compare Rudolf Hermann, *Luthers These "Gerecht und Suender zugleich"* (Guetersloh: 1930), esp. p. 234ff; and J. Haar, *Initium creaturae Dei* (Guetersloh: 1939), p. 70ff. Haar understands the "new life" as "becoming" or as the "Christian's gradual growth (*das zeitliche Fortschreiten*) from baptism to resurrection under the gracious guidance of God" (*ibid.*, p. 88). It must be noted that Hermann's interpretation does not exclude the psychological side of faith, but subordinates it to the time scheme. This has also been shown by W. Joest in his book *Gesetz und Freiheit* (Goettingen: 1951). See especially pp. 82ff; 91ff.

[12] [The original in this and the following sentence has the word *Diener Gottes* as the subject of *Gottesdienst*. Trans.]

ceiving Christ's work through Word and sacrament. For Christ is the true priest of God, and man grows into his likeness as he shares in the priestly work of Christ. Thus Christ overcomes the old man and creates the new. The idolater dies and the worshiper comes forth and rises. Christ himself is the new man. He and the believer are one person.[13]

Luther's continuing emphasis is on the passive character of faith. Faith will never reach that degree of maturity where it could live without receiving. A grateful reception of God's gracious gifts will always remain the task of Christian worship, for it is impossible to evolve a church service out of the spiritual assets of the believers.

In order to undergird this view, we shall consider a few ideas that bear on the meaning of faith and that will help in turn to clarify Luther's picture of worship.

"Passivity" is the mark of the righteousness of faith as contrasted with the righteousness of works which is an "active" righteousness.[14] Here the difference is between a righteousness that God gives, to be received passively by man, and one that he would so infuse into man's soul as to enable him to develop faith from his own spiritual resources.

Luther even spoke of Christian holiness as something passive, for it is the reception of the holiness of God in Christ.[15] The be-

[13] *WA* 7, 469: "To put on Christ is nothing else than to be conformed to his image and example." Luther also develops, in connection with Gal. 2:20, Christ's total rule over the believer as a person. Compare F. Frey, *Luthers Glaubensbegriff. Gottesgabe und Menschentat in ihrer Polaritaet* (Leipzig: 1939), p. 110f and the quotations from the Large Commentary on Galatians given there; also E. Schott, *Fleisch und Geist nach Luthers Lehre* (Leipzig: 1928), p. 40ff.

[14] *WA* 40 I, 41: "For here we do or give nothing to God, but only receive and allow another to work in us—God. This righteousness of faith may therefore be called passive." Cf. 40 I, 42.

[15] *WA* 40 I, 70.

liever can never have or hold a holiness of his very own. He is continually being sanctified by the ongoing work of God. Man's attempt to sanctify himself with works of his own devising is blasphemous and hopeless, for it hinders him from accepting that holiness which God imparts through Word and sacraments.[16] This holiness appears only to the eyes of faith. It does not rest on human qualities and so it remains invisible to human sight. Outwardly the church consists of sinners.[17] Its holiness rests not on the character of its members, but on the continued activity of the Holy Spirit.[18]

Thus justification and sanctification are intimately bound to the worship in Word and sacraments by which God carries out his redemptive work. In no sense is this worship a preparatory stage which faith could ultimately leave behind. Rather faith might be defined as a passive cult *(cultus passivus)* because in this life it will always depend on the worship by which God imparts himself—a gift granted to the believing congregation.

This is confirmed in Luther's explanation of the Third Commandment. To him, sabbath rest[19] meant more than a pause from work. It should be an opportunity for God to do his work on man. God wants to distract man from his daily toil and so open him to God's gifts. To observe the sabbath is not a good work which man could offer to God. On the contrary, it means pausing from all our works and letting God do his work in and for us.[20] From the mystics Luther borrowed the term *Gelassenheit*

[16] *WA* 50, 626; 30 I, 367; 40 I, 69.

[17] *WA* 40I, 444f. Cf. 39I, 165: "Christian perfection consists in the forgiveness of sins."

[18] *WA* 50, 625; 18, 522.

[19] [The German form of the commandment translates sabbath by *Feiertag*. And it must be noted that the German word *Feier* implies both rest from work and an act of worship or celebration. Trans.]

[20] *WA* 1, 436, 437, 440; 6, 244, 247; 35, 427; 30 I, 144; 10 I, 1, 675.

(repose of the soul) to describe this attitude,[21] which he also found in the empty soul *(anima vacua)* of the "poor in spirit."[22] But neither *Gelassenheit* nor "spiritual poverty" refer to a human accomplishment or preparation for the reception of grace *(dispositio ad gratiam)*. They only serve to define that state where God alone is active and man entirely passive.[23] For man's activity must be swept out of heaven where his works count for nothing and be busied instead on earth where his fellow-men wait for him to exercise his Christian faith.[24]

The devil and the flesh resist this spiritual rest, and it takes a struggle to make man relax from his feverish efforts to save himself.[25] Christ himself through his Word and the sacraments must fill his soul with sabbath rest. In order for this to happen, the old Adam must die. "Here one must afflict nature and let it be afflicted."[26] The new man who will rest before God is not born without pain—the death of the old Adam. Here God performs his strange work *(opus alienum)* in order to confound the enemy who would hinder man from being at rest before God.[27]

Luther connected this explanation of the sabbath with Christ's death and his rest in the grave.[28] As Christ died for our sins and

[21] *WA* 1, 254; 10^{II}, 382, 386. Cf. also Frey, *op. cit.*, p. 104f.

[22] *WA* 1, 254, 440.

[23] *WA* 10 ^{II}, 386.

[24] G. Wingren, *Luther on Vocation*, pp. 1-77.

[25] *WA* 6, 244. This struggle against the flesh suggests the need of bodily discipline. Luther speaks of asceticism under the terms *Uebung* (exercise), *Kasteiung des Fleisches* (chastisement of the flesh), and *mortificatio carnis* (mortification of the flesh); compare Ottmar Dittrich, *Luthers Ethik* (Leipzig: 1930), p. 59ff where the difference between Luther and the medieval concept of asceticism is discussed; also G. Ljunggren, *Synd och skuld*, p. 74ff, 118ff; L. Fendt, *Luthers Schule der Heiligung* (Leipzig: 1929), p. 41ff.

[26] *WA* 6, 244.

[27] *WA* 6, 248. See also W. Joest, *op. cit.*, p. 114f.

[28] *WA* 9, 663. See also August Hardeland, *Luthers Katechismusgedanken in ihrer Entwicklung bis zum Jahre 1529* (Guetersloh: 1913), p. 84ff, and Johannes Meyer, *Historischer Kommentar zu Luthers Kleinem Katechismus* (Guetersloh: 1929), p. 208f.

rested in the grave, so we too must die and spiritually keep the sabbath. For his death is ours. We cannot live unless we have died with him. "He who wants to keep the true spiritual sabbath must first die with Christ. . . . But we begin to keep the true sabbath when our old Adam ceases from all his works, reason, will, desire, and lust, all of which shall die and cease in the true sabbath [here there is a quotation from Gal. 2:14f; 6:14]. . . . This sabbath cannot be kept until we are dead."[29] But as God raised Christ, so will he give the new life of the Spirit to those who have wholly died to their own works.

Thus Luther's picture of the sabbath is marked by the passivity of man and the activity of God. And it applies not only to certain holy days of the calendar, but to the Christian life in its entirety, testifying to man's existence as a creature of God who waits by faith for the life to come.[30] Through God's activity in Christ, man is drawn into the death and resurrection of the Redeemer and so recreated a new man in Christ. The Third Commandment lays on us no obligation for specific works of any sort (not even spiritual or cultic works) but rather directs us to the work of God. And we do not come into contact with the latter except in the service, where Christ meets us in the means of grace.

Faith as Hearing the Word and Using the Sacrament

Two ideas will occupy us in this section: faith by hearing *(fides ex auditu)* and the use of the sacrament *(usus sacramenti)*.

We begin with the idea of faith by hearing which Luther found in Romans 10:-17. His early lectures on Hebrews develop this concept in a manner that is typical of his whole approach.[31]

[29] *WA* 16, 480, 481.

[30] *WA* 1, 436; 30^{I}, 145; 42, 61.

[31] For the following compare Eduard Ellwein, "Die Entfaltung der theologia crucis in Luthers Hebräerbriefvorlesung," *Karl Barth Festschrift* (Muenchen: 1936), p. 391ff.

To hear the Word is to believe and be justified and is the only mark which entitles man to call himself a Christian.[32] Faith points entirely beyond itself, beyond the work of men toward a righteousness which is not our own. It is a clinging to the word given to us *(adhaesio verbi Dei)*.[33] The man of faith hears nothing but this voice. He stands on the foundation of the external Word. This Word, as it penetrates his heart, transforms it and makes him a child of God. It is therefore the hearing of the Word more than anything else that characterizes faith in the theology of Luther.[34]

Since faith comes by hearing, it depends on worship. It is bound to God as he offers himself to men. In this connection it must be noted that Luther did not try to describe the act of hearing psychologically. Hearing is not a work of man to prepare himself for grace, but an entirely passive attitude.[35] It is simply being addressed and arrested by the voice of God. As a matter of fact Luther made "hearing" synonymous with "preaching" when he translated Romans 10:17 as *"So kommt der Glaube aus der Predigt"* (Thus faith comes by preaching). His idea of preaching included the listener. The essence of the Word is challenge *(Anrede)*. To be a man is to live by this challenge of the Word of God.[36] This explains his emphasis on the "external" Word from the pulpit and his rejection of the "inner" Word of the Enthusiasts, for the man who is concerned about his own ability to hear has ceased to listen to the Word of God, and is lost in the vain attempt to assess his own devotion and attentiveness.[37]

[32] *WA* 57, 222.
[33] *WA* 57, 228 (Hb); 57, 139 (Hb); 57, 151 (Hb); 27, 399.
[34] *WA* 57, 149, 156, 147, 151 (Hb); 40 I, 361; 10 I, 48.
[35] *WA* 6, 216; 40 I, 243.
[36] *WA* 51, 11. This is the main emphasis of G. Wingren's book *Predikan*.
[37] *WA* 30 I, 215.

Faith according to Luther is dominated by God's own work (the sermon). But it is in grave danger of becoming a human work (for example, a psychological achievement), as soon as the Lutheran equation of sermon-plus-hearing-equals-faith is lost sight of. Luther marks this fact by contrasting a supposed "inner hearing" and "inner word" with the "outward word" of the orally delivered sermon.[38]

Luther was therefore far from spiritualizing the meaning of worship when he said that faith is the true worship. For faith is bound to the eternal Word of God. It links the call of God with man who has been created for the Word and who lives by hearing.

Hearing is not an isolated act which might lead to faith, but a continued acceptance of life from God.[39] Wherever men are open to the Word of God, there is the church.[40]

Earlier we stressed the "for-us" character of the Sacrament. As the congregation shares Christ's presence-for-us, the Sacrament is used. More specifically, it is by faith that we can rightly use the Sacrament. And to receive it without faith means to abuse it.[41] Through faith it becomes effectual, that is, it imparts remission of sins as pledged in the Words of Institution.[42] Using the Sacrament in faith means to be open to the work of God and so to be incorporated into Christ.[43] Unbelief does not escape the Lord, but eats and drinks damnation to itself *(manducatio infidelium)*,[44] for the use does not constitute the Sacrament. It only indicates

[38] *WA* 30 I, 215.
[39] R. Prenter, *op. cit.,* p. 119.
[40] *WA* 11, 408.
[41] *WA* 2, 695, 742.
[42] *WA* 57, 169 (Hb) ; 2, 715; 6, 371 ; 1, 324; 6, 361, 471, etc.
[43] This is stressed especially in the Communion Sermon of 1519, but it also is found in many other passages, as for example *WA* 18, 168; 19, 509.
[44] *WA* 6, 502; 18, 194; 23, 179; 26, 287.

that we receive the gift of God under the bread and wine, while unbelief consists in the refusal or denial of the gift of God.[45]

All this implies the importance of the promise. Faith comes by preaching, and the elements must be comprehended in the Word in order to inspire faith. Nay, though a man should be denied access to the altar, he still could use the Sacrament simply by faith in the Words of Institution.[46] But normally the Sacrament should be received not only with the ear, but with the mouth as well. Luther increasingly stressed the importance of communion as essential to the Sacrament.[47]

The belief that Christ is present in the bread and wine to be consumed by the communicants was an offense to the Enthusiasts. They could accept an "inner," "spiritual" eating, but not an "outward," "bodily" reception. Luther opposed this "spiritualism" on the basis of the First Article. God claims not only the soul and

[45] Karl Barth's fatal misinterpretation of Luther's early statements about faith as constitutive for the effect of the Sacrament (*Ansatz und Absicht in Luthers Abendmahlslehre,* p. 36ff) comes from the fact that he interprets Luther on the basis of a philosophy foreign to the Reformer—the premise that there can be no sacrament without faith (For Luther, this would amount to the claim that apart from faith, God and his redemptive acts do not exist). But here too, Luther must be interpreted on the basis of his "dualistic" approach which implies that the Sacrament without faith becomes a curse, for it is abused by unbelief. This is what Luther means when he says that "the sacrament without faith effects nothing" (cited by Barth, p. 37). The "effect" and "profit" which Luther denies in the passages quoted by Barth are effect and profit *for salvation*. But Luther did not deny an evil effect in the unbelieving reception of the Sacrament. Luther's thought in these passages parallels his exposition of the famous phrase *glaubst du, so hast du* (to believe is to have). Cf. the passage quoted by Barth, p. 42, note 70 where this connection is emphasized. Luther's later writings against the Enthusiasts are quite in line with his earlier thoughts on the sacraments and serve only to unfold what he had taught before. Barth's ironical comment, "Long before Zwingli had risen, Luther had given sufficient arguments—against himself" (p. 37, n. 53), might better be modified to read: "Long before Zwingli [and why not also Barth?] had risen, Luther had given sufficient arguments against him [and against Barth]." Compare the Luther passages quoted in the last footnote.

[46] *WA* 6, 532, 533.

[47] *WA* 23, 179; 26, 296; 30 I, 388ff. Cf. 30 II, 599.

"inner self," but the whole man, body, soul, and spirit. Even the body, though unconscious of the benefit received, is to share in the blessing.[48] And contrariwise the soul cannot partake inwardly and spiritually without the outward, visible gift out of the paten and the cup.[49]

Of course, eating and drinking without faith is of no avail.[50] But neither can faith be divorced from bread and wine. The dividing line between inward and outward, spiritual and carnal eating is between eating and drinking with faith (inward, spiritual eating) or without it (outward, carnal eating). In the first case, man is the "inner man" (spirit); in the second, the "outer man" (flesh).[51] A third or neutral option does not exist.[52]

Even the abstention from the Supper does not exempt a man from the decision between faith and unbelief, for by refusing to commune, he has despised the gift of Christ. Some may indeed be kept away by religious scruples. The very sincerity of their faith may bring their unworthiness to mind. But Luther answered them by pointing out that the Word and Sacrament do not rest on our worthiness.[53] Rather, our worthiness rests on the Word and on the Sacrament. Faith is not a condition that man must

[48] *WA* 23, 191.

[49] *WA* 17 II, 132; 23, 181. Cf. E. Sommerlath, *Der Sinn des Abendmahls*, p. 73f.

[50] *WA* 26, 353.

[51] R. Bring elucidates the antinomy "inward" versus "outward" from the two different kinds of righteousness and presents Luther's changing terminology with its differing emphases in a theological scheme. The problem within Luther's view of the church that we are concerned with is only one phase within that larger connection.

[52] A "memorial supper" unrelated to God and worship is really an abuse of the sacrament.

[53] *WA* 2, 694; 30 I, 230: "The only kind of worthiness is that which accepts the promise of God." That is why Luther criticized the communion prayer of the priest in the mass *"Domine, non sum dignus"* (Lord, I am not worthy, etc.) in 7, 694: "A man should beware of coming on account of his own worthiness; nor should he pray for the latter, as some do who pray

fulfil apart from Word and sacraments, but the gift which God imparts through these means of grace.[54]

The quest for worthiness tends to misdirect our faith. Man no longer thinks of himself as resting from his works, nor of God as active and forgiving sins.[55] The worthiness of man is made a pawn by which to claim the grace of God.[56] This is a perversion of faith. The certainty of our salvation rests, not upon faith as an accomplishment of man, but upon the unmotivated love of God imparting worth to him who of himself is totally unworthy.[57]

Thus the *usus sacramenti* rests not on personal worthiness, but on the work of God, for faith (worthiness) is built on the fact that God in Christ is present to impart life eternal. Blessing comes only from the promise of the Word. Let the weak in faith cling to the Word and seek neither worthiness nor unworthiness within himself.[58] Any claim of worthiness to motivate the gift of God is an attempt to escape both the judgment and forgiveness of God. We have no life except in the continuing advent of Christ in Word and sacrament. So to rest from our works that we might be conformed to his death is faith. Thus faith is the only kind of worthiness, while unbelief makes us unworthy,[59] for faith sees nothing in itself but sin and death, that is, unworthiness. But in the midst of hell it hears a voice inspiring hope in the Creator, who can create the new man in Christ out of nothing.[60]

the verse, 'Lord, I am not worthy that thou shouldst enter under my roof, but say in a word, and my soul shall be healed.' Not that I condemn this prayer; but one should cling to something much closer, namely, the words by which Christ instituted the mass and says, Take and eat, etc."

[54] *WA* 2, 686; 6, 521; 8, 437; 18, 200.

[55] *WA* 11, 448.

[56] *WA* 8, 357.

[57] *WA* 1, 354; 40 I, 344. Cf. A. Nygren, *Agape and Eros*, p. 724f.

[58] *WA* 6, 158, 362.

[59] *WA* 2, 693; 1, 255.

[60] Creation out of nothing (*creatio ex nihilo*) is stressed by G. Wingren in *Luther on Vocation*, pp. 183-4; and by R. Prenter who (*op. cit.*, pp. 183-4) links this thought to the Holy Spirit's recreating power.

Faith has no other certainty but the proclamation of the Word and the administration of the sacraments.[61] This Word must be heard and this Sacrament received in the assurance that he who imparts the body and blood is the Risen Lord.

Thus faith through hearing and the use of the Sacrament are linked so closely that they differ not in the nature of the gift received, but only in its outer form. Here it is a voice heard and taken to heart, there bread and wine received while the same voice is heard. But this difference in the form of the gift can become helpful in the hour of temptation *(Anfechtung)*.[62] For the sermon speaks to the congregation as a whole. Every listener is expected to apply the message to himself. But the one who is troubled in conscience finds it hard to do this. He needs the Sacrament by which God says to him "for you." There he receives the assurance that he is not being passed over by the Lord. The Sacrament bridges the gap between Christ's salvation revealed and offered to all and the lonely individual in his spiritual need, for as he hears the words "for you," he eats and drinks and so is assured—not of his worthiness, but of the work of God who out of nothing makes him anew a man of faith.[63]

Ambiguity and Christological Unity in the Theology of Worship

Luther's insistence on the importance to faith of the external means of grace would be misinterpreted if it was made to imply an identification of faith with the hearing of the Word or the reception of the sacraments. This would amount to identifying

[61] *WA* 1, 255.

[62] Paul T. Buehler, *Die Anfechtung bei Luther* (Zuerich: 1942), p. 102ff. [It is almost impossible to render the German word *Anfechtung* by a single English word. The temptations to which it refers are spiritual, rather than carnal, doubts of God's love, scruples of conscience, etc. Trans.]

[63] This applies also to the absolution as a personal pledge of the forgiveness in Christ. See for example *WA* 15, 486f.

the worshiping congregation with the communion of saints. Faith would be reduced to a certain cultic attitude and the church to the people who observe the same. But it is this very attitude that Luther sought to forestall by his emphasis on faith as the proper worship. How then could he so strongly stress the connection of faith with the external means of grace and yet refuse simply to identify the external acts of worship with the true worship of faith? This question is intimately linked with what Luther has to say about the visibility and invisibility of the church.

Luther liked to speak of the church as invisible, spiritual, and inward.[64] The invisibility of the church follows from its nature as the "communion of saints."[65] The church is the people of God.[66] However, though Luther developed his picture of the invisible church in opposition to the Roman dogma of a visible outward church,[67] it does not follow that he rejected ecclesiastical ceremonies and laws as such and embraced a spiritualistic view of the church. This is how Rudolf Sohm interpreted Luther. But Sohm confused the view of the Enthusiasts with that of Luther. Luther's premise regarding the contrast of spiritual versus physical and invisible versus visible was totally different from that of the Enthusiasts.[68]

[64] *WA* 1, 639; 6, 64, 292ff; 7, 710.

[65] Besides the passages referred to above, see also *WA* 11, 53; 30 I, 92, 189; 50, 250, 624ff.

[66] *WA* 50, 625.

[67] See the passages in n. 64 above. In *Von dem Papsttum* (*WA* 6, 297ff) Luther rejects the Roman idea of the church which links the church to outward places, bodily attitudes, etc. This is a threat to the spiritual, invisible, and inward unity which rests exclusively on the faith. See also *WA* 7, 710.

[68] Not even Luther's *Von dem Papsttum* betrays a spiritualistic view, although here the dividing line between internal and external Christendom is most clearly marked. Some remarks imply a connection between outward and inward Christendom (*WA* 6, 296, 297) but it is not discussed any further in this work. Cf. G. Aulén, *Till belysning av den lutherska kyrkoiden* (Uppsala: 1912), p. 40. To Rudolph Sohm the church is invisible only. Insofar as it has outward marks (*notae ecclesiae*) it is not the church but the "Christian world."

The church is invisible, but it is not thereby removed from the visible world of creation. On the contrary, the invisible is found in the visible, the spiritual under the material, and the inward within the outward.[69] Though invisible, the church is marked by the external means of grace, which can be heard and seen, tasted and felt. Thus we come to a problem similar to the one noted above with reference to worship: How is it possible to maintain on the one hand the connection of an invisible church (of faith) with the visible means of grace and on the other to reject the uncritical identification of the two?[70] Faith is indeed invisible.

This completely cuts off the church from the created world; the church becomes a spiritualistic idea. The tension between the external (visible) and internal (spiritual) is understood in a way quite different from that in Luther's theology. See Rudolph Sohm, "Kirchenrecht," in *Systematisches Handbuch der deutschen Rechtswissenschaft* (Leipzig: 1923), II, especially p. 130ff, and Edmund Schlink's criticism in "Theologie der Bekenntnisschriften," in *Einfuehrung in die evangelische Theologie* (Muenchen: 1946), VIII, p. 269f, n. 301.

[69] It is characteristic of Luther's thought that he applies the opposites "invisible-visible" to one and the same object. He did not think of two churches, nor of two concentric circles, the larger of which would correspond to the visible and the smaller to the invisible church. Schematically one can distinguish two groups of attributes in Luther's idea of the church:

1. invisible—spiritual—internal
2. visible—physical (*leiblich*)—external

It is characteristic of Luther: 1) that the attributes noted above are used simultaneously, expressing the nature of the church in a unity marked by tension. This must be understood on the basis of Luther's doctrine of the Holy Spirit who is always found in the external things of creation. 2) that the attributes of group 1 appear as expressing the true nature of the church, while the attributes of group 2 (isolated from group 1) are rejected. This rejection must be interpreted as the rejection of an aspect that would contradict the totality aspect (1 and 2) and so isolate one group of attributes at the expense of the other. This can be exemplified from both the Roman and the Enthusiasts' ideas of the church. Rome would single out 2 and make the church visible, physical, external. The Enthusiasts stress 1 exclusively without considering that men live within creation and that they receive the Holy Spirit through the means of creation and not through a spirituality divorced from creation. The problem of the visible or invisible church reflects the changing terminology of external-internal as charted by R. Bring (see above p. 136, n. 51).

[70] Of newer works on Luther's view of the church, compare Herbert Olsson, "The Church's Visibility and Invisibility according to Luther," in Nygren, *This Is the Church*, p. 226ff.

But it is linked to visible things. It includes a human act as part of God's. Far from seeking an escape from human existence, it is human existence at its truest.[71]

The same applies to the church as the communion of saints *(communio sanctorum)*. Though invisible, it does not transcend the earthly sphere. As a fellowship its external marks are worship, the proclamation of the Word, and the administration of the sacraments.[72] In a sense the communion of saints is the worshiping congregation. Yet it cannot be defined in attendance statistics, for it is the fellowship of believers (saints), of those who share the work of God by faith.[73] In this sense the church includes no hypocrites, none who abuse the Word and sacraments by unbelief.[74] At this point we seem to encounter in Luther's theology a dualism that cannot be reduced to a common denominator.

On one hand church and worship appear to be identical with the proclamation of the Word and the administration of the sacraments. And as mankind belongs to the Word proclaimed and the sacraments administered, church and worship seem to concern and include all of humanity. Faith or unbelief seem to make no difference. Church and worship are the works by which he deals with unbelieving men. They belong to the warfare through which Christ establishes faith among them.

On the other hand, church and worship appear to be the works

[71] *WA* 40 I, 345.

[72] Luther also expressed this in his *Von dem Papsttum,* a work that is problematical to many scholars (*WA* 6, 301). In order to preclude a spiritualistic misinterpretation it might be well to speak of the "hiddenness" rather than the "invisibility" of the church. See H. Olsson, "The Church's Visibility and Invisibility." Here "hiddenness" is used mostly as an expression of God's action within the things of creation.

[73] Faith holds to the promise of Isaiah 55:11 and therewith to the assurance that the church of Christ must be where the Word has free course. *WA* 10 I, 2, 50; 11, 408, etc.

[74] *WA* 6, 297; 50, 625. Compare G. Aulén, *Till belysning av den lutherska kyrkoiden,* p. 35ff, and R. Sohm, "Kirchenrecht," I, p. 465f; II, p. 135.

of faith, of redeemed humanity. Here faith is the essential. The church is the communion of believers and the service the expression of their faith. Unbelief stands outside of the church and its worship, for it represents the devil's "church" and idolatry. Faith (as church and worship) is righteousness, holiness, redemption, and eternal life. Unbelief is unrighteousness, sin, damnation, and death. Christ and his people are the only ones who are entitled to the name of church or who are fit to worship God in spirit and in truth. This dualism in Luther's theology is the reason for the wide divergence among his interpreters. By some the church is viewed as an institute for the proclamation of the Word and the administration of the sacraments, by others as a fellowship of believers, a congregation.[75] Similarly, worship is conceived by some as an institute for the conversion and training of unbelievers and the weak in faith (pedagogical view), by others as the worshiper's expression of his faith (re-presentative view).

But a one-sided presentation cannot do justice to Luther, not even to the particular side of his theology on which it lays stress. Nor is it possible to explain this dualism on the basis of the fact that faith as something inward and invisible cannot be demonstrated except within the outward and visible things in which it is hidden. For it is more than an expedient. It lies at the root of Luther's theology. The solution lies deeper and must be found in the basic structure of his thought.

At this point it is necessary to recall the two lines which form the hidden counterpoint of Luther's theology and on which we based our presentation: the theme of God and that of faith.

On the one hand, we presented worship as the ministry of God *(Dienst Gottes)* in and by which he comes to men. In this aspect,

[75] See Fagerberg, *op. cit.*, especially chap. IV, p. 195ff.

worship is the work by which God continues his creative activity. He does his work unmindful of the faith or unbelief of human office-bearers or of the receiving congregation, for the Word is God's and the Sacrament Christ's body and blood, regardless of the faith of the recipients. Worship is the institute by which God through the Holy Spirit carries on his salutary work and inspires faith in men.

On the other hand, we viewed worship through the aspect of faith. This implied a sharp distinction between faith and unbelief, for in this view there can be no worship without faith. Man is considered, not as an officiant *(Amtsperson)* or instrument of God, but as the individual *(Einzelperson)* with whom God deals.[76] In his personal character, faith or unbelief is the essential. External hearing or receiving is not enough. But a man's personal faith constitutes his worship. Without faith, God's work confers nothing but eternal condemnation. *Glaubst du, so hast du. . . .*[77]

But "these two belong together—faith and God." The two lines that mark Luther's picture of worship must intersect at some

[76] Luther's idea of personality is marked by the twofold relation to God and to the neighbor. This is expressed in the terms Christ-person, individual person, as well as world-person and person-in-office. See H. Olsson, *Grundproblemet i Luthers socialetik,* I, p. 202ff.

[77] In as early a work as Luther's Commentary on Romans (in a gloss on Rom. 3:25) we find the explanation: "Christ 'whom God hath set forth' (ordained from eternity and now set forth) 'a propitiation through faith' (so that he should be a propitiation, but only for the believers, for by unbelief the propitiation is changed to a tribunal and judgment)" (*WA* 56, 38). 18, 195: "The Word of God is always salutary, although to the godless it is a poison and a savor of death unto death." Here belongs the question of the *manducatio indignorum,* communion of the unworthy. See *WA* 26, 353: "I have taught and still teach about the flesh of Christ, not alone that it profiteth nothing, but even that it is poison and death when eaten without the Word and faith. More than that, I have said that God and the Holy Ghost himself is nothing but poison and death and of no avail when received without faith. . . ." In a sermon on Matthew 12:1-8 (Christ as the Lord of the Sabbath), Luther discusses the reasons why the liberty of Christ, by which he freed men from the ritual law, was an offense to the Jews (37, 571ff [Roerer]). He offers an explanation with the help of the frequently cited passage from Ps. 18:25f. It is the same Christ who is a God to the one and a devil to the other (37, 576).

point. A christological solution suggests itself. In his *Von dem Papsttum* Luther in a controversy with the "Romanist" Alveld expounded the difference between Christ's biblical titles, "Head" and "Lord." He is the Lord of all men, both evil and good, but he is also the Head of the body (the church) and as such belongs only to the believers. As the Head of the church he is the same as the Lord of the world. But his "headship" implies that his lordship has been accepted by faith, that he is "my Lord," and that his kingdom "comes to us."

"Christ is indeed the Lord of all things, of good and bad, of angels and devils, of virgins and harlots, but he is not the Head except of devout, believing Christians, gathered in the Spirit. A head belongs organically to its body, as I have proved from Ephesians 4, and the members must depend on the head and have their function and life from him. Therefore Christ cannot be the head of an evil crowd, although the latter is subject to him as Lord. Even so his kingdom, Christendom, is not an outward body or kingdom, yet everything is subject to him, whether spiritual or material, heavenly or hellish." [78]

This distinction can be applied to Luther's view of worship. For worship is God's spiritual rule (lordship) through the Word and sacrament. Faith and unbelief live under the same Lord, but it is only faith which acknowledges him. Faith makes the work of God its own. It creates no new world, but lives in the one created and ruled by God. It adds nothing to the work of God, effects no change in reality, but makes man a new person.[79]

[78] *WA* 6, 301. Cf. 14, 22. With the idea of Christ as the Head belongs the idea of faith as the proper use of pronouns (*WA* 40 I, 85f, 9, 299). This distinguishes true faith from mere "historical" faith (*WA* 39 I, 446). Prayer likewise belongs here (see the whole explanation of the Lord's Prayer in the Small Catechism, especially *WA* 30 I, 371).

[79] The recreating power of faith is associated with the renewal of man's personality. Through the same reality which to unbelief appeared as a

Unbelief, on the contrary, faces the same reality. It also exists under the reign, spiritual and secular, of God, for the devil cannot create anything. But like the tyrant he is, he wants to alienate man from God and cause him to rebel against the Lord of heaven and earth. Man's sin lies in the presumption that he could make himself lord of creation. He attempts to create new gods and new ways of worship. But he succeeds only in making idols and idolatries, for the figments of his own making have nothing to do with him who actually rules the world, nor with his will and Word. Man cannot be a true worshiper or minister of God (*Diener Gottes*) except by a passive faith content to receive the works of God, claiming no merit of his own before the throne on high.

Faith retains the bond between the Lord and individual man. Unbelief, though cutting man loose from God, cannot escape the rule and reach of God.

Thus the connection between worship as the work of God (God's lordship) and as the work of faith (personal fellowship with God) may be summarized in the following propositions:

(1) The worship of faith is of grace, not of merit. It is a gift from God and not our work for him. It is Christ present for our salvation in the Word and sacraments, Christ not as a virtue within man but as God "for us."

(2) Unbelief, far from being a retreat into a neutral sphere, remote from God, is idolatry, and as such is a judgment over the apostasy of evil men. Nor can unbelief escape the form of wor-

revelation of the wrath of God, the love of God flows into the life of man. See Wingren, *Luther on Vocation,* p. 145. R. Johannesson (in *Person och gemenskap*) points out in his disagreement with Wingren that faith must not be made the condition for the application of God's love toward the individual (p. 193, n. 29). To this we must reply that God indeed meets all mankind with his love, but that he is known as the God of love only through the renewing power of faith. Faith cannot be called a "condition" unless it is understood as an effort of man instead of a work of the Holy Spirit.

ship by which God rules his kingdom through the Word, for it is the Word that trips him.

This apostasy through unbelief is a universal condition among men. Grace can never be alone, but must be linked with the forgiveness of our sins. It includes judgment over idolatry. This judgment no one can escape. No one can become a worshiper or minister of God (*Diener Gottes*) without first being judged as an idolater. Christ present in worship must overcome the idolatry of unbelief. Through his strange work, the judgment on idolatry, God grants his proper work, worship by faith through grace. Faith accepts this twofold work of God and so "has" God. Unbelief tries vainly to "possess" the Lord by shirking his judgment on idolatry. Therefore true worship implies a constant struggle of faith with unbelief.

The line between faith and unbelief cannot be drawn as between two classes of men, for the believer himself stands under judgment for his lack of faith and lives alone by God's continued work of salvation. This earth is the battleground where the captives of the devil are redeemed by Christ. Faith and unbelief are still existing side by side, for the Last Day has not come. Good and evil, true disciples and idolaters, those who worship God in truth and hypocrites, all are living under the rule of God through Word and sacrament. Judgment (God's wrath) and grace (God's love) as the twofold work of God both concern all of mankind and one and the same man in it, for his worship consists in being judged and redeemed by Christ *(von Christus gerichtet und gerade so aufgerichtet zu werden).*

Here is the answer to the question why the external act (hearing the Word and using the sacraments) cannot simply be identified with the internal yet belongs to it, even as the invisible church (faith) is not identical with the worshiping congregation, though it belongs to it. The external act is God's activity and can be used with or without faith. Man is included in the work of God as a fellow-worker (co-operator, office-bearer, preacher) or recipient of the gift (of the Word and sacrament). But he is always apt to abuse the external act by unbelief. The old Adam tends to make a meritorious work of the external act. He wants to raise himself above God. And so he not only remains in idolatry, but becomes more evil through the external work.

The struggle between faith and unbelief takes place within one and the same world made by God. It is not the external act (the works) in itself that makes the difference between faith and unbelief. Actually, from a theological viewpoint there is no such act in itself. Otherwise we could manipulate God by our way of handling created things. But God, while not beyond the created world, is over it. That is why worship and the church of faith are linked to the externals of the created world without being identical with them, for faith is not of the earth, but of heaven.

It will now be seen why Luther based faith so firmly on the Word and sacraments, and at the same time so violently criticized the canons of the Roman church by which men were obliged to hear the mass and were yet denied the preaching of the faith which alone could make the Sacrament a blessing for them. For without faith he found nothing in the mass but idolatry and eternal condemnation rather than profit in attending it.[80]

But where faith is preached, and worship is presented as the gracious gift of God, men are led gladly and thankfully to receive the gifts of God in Word and sacrament,[81] for such faith is worship, an offering of thanks for God's gift of his kingdom

[80] *WA* 30 II, 598; 6, 230, 207; 8, 168; 19, 73; 2, 757.
[81] *WA* 30 II, 600; 6, 378.

"for me." It is by faith that God's saving work becomes his service through Christ "for me" and so becomes "my" service through Christ before God.

This application to the individual of the work of God transcends rational analysis.[82] It can be classed with the gift of the Holy Ghost. The Spirit comes by the means of grace. But he is not so confined to them that man can control or call him up. For the Spirit we can only wait.[83] Ultimately, faith which waits for the works of God and rests from its own may learn through the Holy Spirit the true experience of worshiping God. True worship is thanksgiving. At the same time, it submits to God's judgment and so experiences God's redeeming love in the opposite form *(sub contraria specie)*. Thus faith's thanksgiving is always a sacrifice of thanks, as the old man dies and the new one comes forth. The following chapter will treat this twofold aspect of the new worship of faith.

[82] Cf. Luther's explanation of the Third Article in the Small Catechism, 30 I, 367.

[83] Prenter, *op. cit.*, p. 122ff. See also the passages from Luther quoted on p. 250, n. 2, pp. 256f, 258, where the sovereignty of the Holy Spirit is stressed. He links the sovereignty of the Spirit to the predestination emphasis in the theology of Luther.

7

The Priestly Sacrifice of Believers

Luther considered the priesthood in the context of redemptive history. Under the Old Covenant he found an external priesthood, the line of priests descended from Aaron and whose task it was to go with external sacrifices between God and his people.[1] But this Levitical priesthood and its laws had become obsolete with Christ; for—and here is the rub—it was no more than a "type" of Christ.[2] Aaron typified the true high priest who would fulfil the promise. The task of the Levitical priesthood was to prefigure Christ.

Priesthood and Sacrifice

With the coming of Christ, the priesthood was transformed, for Christ himself has become both priest and sacrifice. The priesthood of the New Testament has a single priest who mediates between God and man.[3] In the fulness of time, he came and rendered a unique sacrifice. He gave himself and suffered death upon the cross. This sacrifice was not for himself for he was without sin but for those whose condemnation by the law he suffered, whose sins he bore, whose guilt he cancelled, and for whom he opened the way to God.

[1] *WA* 8, 485: "Of all the priesthoods, two are truly and divinely instituted. One is the Levitical where the high priest was Aaron, the law the books of Moses, the sacrifices cattle and material things. . . . The other priesthood is Christian and spiritual where the eternal, living, and holy Christ alone is the high priest."

[2] *WA* 8, 394. Cf. 57, 165 (Hb) and 166 (Hb).

[3] *WA* 8, 415, 417; 57, 190 (Exegesis of Heb. 7:12).

The vicarious character of his work implies that all those for whom he suffered are included in his priesthood.[4] All who receive the Lord by faith are priests of the New Covenant. Here is the foundation for the priesthood of all believers.[5] As Christ is a priest, so is every Christian who clings to him in faith. Christ and the Christians belong together, and faith is the true priesthood.[6] Christ shares everything with those who believe in him. As he is the Son, the Heir, and the true High Priest, so the believers are sons of God, heirs, and priests.[7] In the position of recipients (in faith), they stand before the great High Priest, by whose priesthood alone they are able to serve God, as they offer themselves with Christ and for their fellow-men. To be a priest under the New Covenant is to be both a "priest with Christ" and a "priest for the neighbor."[8]

Luther based the priesthood of all believers on the "royal priesthood" of I Peter 2:9 and on Revelation 1:6, 5:10, and 20:6 ("priests of God and of Christ"). To "be a priest" equals in biblical language to "believe in Christ" and to "be a Christian." The title "priest" is common to all Christians. The new birth which comes by baptism and faith consecrates them priests in the kingdom of God. "The Holy Spirit in the New Testament carefully avoids applying the name of priest *(Sacerdos* or *Pfaffe)* to any of the apostles or any other office. It is solely the name of the baptized or Christians."[9] "For under the New Testament now

[4] *WA* 8, 415.
[5] *WA* 8, 415; 8, 422; 12, 179. See Goesta Hoek, "Luthers laera om kyrkans aembete," in *En bok om kyrkans aembete* (Stockholm: 1951), p. 151ff.
[6] *WA* 6, 370.
[7] *WA* 7, 56 (I Pet. 2:9). See also 12, 179.
[8] *WA* 7, 57; 57, 166 (Hb). Cf. 16, 406 (Roerer) and especially 407. See V. Vajta, "Der Christenstand als 'koenigliches Priestertum,'" in Nygren, *Welt-Luthertum von heute* (Stockholm: 1950), especially pp. 350, 360. 367ff.
[9] *WA* 38, 230. Cf. 7, 57f; 8, 253, 416; 12, 178; 6, 408, 564; 38, 229.

valid, a priest is not made but born, not ordained but created. He is born not by a birth of the flesh but of the Spirit, of water and the Spirit by the washing of regeneration."[10]

By the same token, Luther rejected the Roman priesthood and the substitution of an episcopal anointing for the spiritual unction of faith. The New Testament priesthood is in the personal dimension. It is not an office. In the form of an office, the Christian church has ministers, but no priests. A priesthood implies sacrifices. As the "external" priesthood of the Old Testament had its sacrifices, so has the "inward" priesthood of the New Testament. This sacrifice is its "reasonable service." Luther liked to quote Romans 12:1 as well as references from the Psalter to the sacrifice of praise (also Heb. 13:15 and I Peter 2:5, 9).[11] Notwithstanding his determined elimination of the sacrificial element from the Lord's Supper, he was careful to preserve the proper biblical picture of sacrifice. Earlier we pointed out that far from neglecting the idea of sacrifice Luther meant only to assign the proper place to it.[12]

The point of reference for the idea of sacrifice in Luther's theology is the priesthood of all believers. Sacrifice is an element of faith. Luther never forgot this fact, even in his most violent polemics against the Roman perversion of sacrifice.[13] But as

[10] *WA* 12, 178. Cf. 12, 317; 17 II, 6.

[11] The most important references are *WA* 6, 369; 8, 420; 12, 185, 306ff, 316; 17 II, 6ff, etc.

[12] Compare above page 44. Luther used the term "sacrifice" consistently in his exegesis of Romans 12:1, interpreting it in accordance with evangelical principles. On the other hand, he tended to apply the theological meaning of "sacrifice" also to other terms, as, for example, that of mortification. He knew what he was doing. Cf. for example *WA* Br. 5, 574 where he points out that Augustine avoided the term *fatum* (fate), although he might have given a positive interpretation to it.

[13] Compare the article by W. Thomas, "Das eucharistische Opfer nach dem lutherischen Bekenntnis," in *Deo omnium unum* (Muenchen: 1942), p. 287.

sacrifice is a function of faith, it cannot be without faith. Luther rejected the Roman theology of the mass for the very reason that it was a conception of sacrifice apart from faith (*ex opere operato*). To him, the mass was a sacrifice only insofar as it was "used" by faith. This is the significance of the sacrifice of Christ (and consequently also of the sacrifice of Christians). "Though the body and blood of Christ was seen like any other material thing, it was not seen as a sacrifice, nor as something he was offering. . . . Christ sacrificed himself to God in his own heart, of which nobody knew. That is why his physical body and blood are a spiritual sacrifice. Likewise we Christians sacrifice our bodies (Rom. 12:1), yet it is, as Paul himself says, a reasonable service, for we do it in the spirit where God alone can see." [14] It is not the officiant who renders sacrifice, for the sacrifice concerns not man in his official capacity *(Amtsperson)*[15] but man as a believer (Christ-person), that is, the receiving congregation.[16]

What is the sacrifice that is related to faith? Luther points to the sacrifice of praise and thanksgiving, of prayer, of the body. He thought of man in all his relationships. His picture of sacrifice is expressive of the total claim of faith.

Sacrifice is associated with death, "for what is to be sacrificed has to be killed."[17] The Christian as a priest offers himself. The victim to be sacrificed is he himself,[18] or, to be more correct, the "old man," the "old Adam" within. In this priestly service, man concurs with the office of the law, for as the law was given to

[14] *WA* 17 II, 228. [15] *Ibid.*

[16] It goes without saying that the officiant too can be a recipient, but only for his own person and not for others, for faith is personal and untransferable. Everyone sacrifices and believes for himself, the officiant not excepted.

[17] *WA* 17 II, 8.

[18] *WA* 17 II, 11: "By the word 'body,' St. Paul refers to everything that has not been reborn of the Spirit, and to the best and highest power of the 'old man,' both outwardly and inwardly." Cf. 8, 420; 12, 185; 49, 212.

uncover sin and to condemn it in the flesh,[19] so the Christian as a priest surrenders his own sinful nature into death.

This sacrifice, when brought by faith, makes him conformable to Christ, for Christ himself submitted to the curse of sin and death and shared man's life and death under the law. But his very humiliation and death resulted in victory.[20] By the same token there shines the star of life and hope over the sacrifice of the believer,[21] for it is in union with Christ that he suffers the condemnation of the law.

Thus Luther's concept of mortification must not be confused with ascetic exercises. These, far from excluding unbelief and work righteousness, may easily be the expression of a completely egocentric religion. This would be the exact opposite of sacrifice.[22] True sacrifice does not consist in man's presenting anything to God. It is effected through Christ.[23] It is the judgment passed on man with all that he may wish to present to God.

Indeed the old man must be killed and crucified with Christ. Sacrifice as dying with Christ is an expression of that strange work of God by which he grants life through death.[24] Since even as a Christian, man must die in order to live, nothing is found in him which could motivate the new life from God. Yet the latter is hidden under death, for the death which the Christian suffers

[19] *WA* 17 II, 9; 12, 185.
[20] *WA* 2, 147. On the basis of Phil. 2:5ff, the humiliation (*exinanitio*) of Christ plays a significant role in Luther's theology. The sermon quoted here is based on this text.
[21] See *WA* 12, 370f, where the thought of a blessed interchange between Christ, the true High Priest, and Christians as priests is developed. Recent Luther research has frequently given attention to the conformity between Christians and Christ, without however linking it to the priesthood and sacrifice of Christians. For a reference to this idea compare H. Olsson, *Grundproblemet i Luthers socialetik*, I, p. 184f.
[22] *WA* 12, 309. Cf. G. Ljunggren, *op. cit.*, p. 75ff.
[23] *WA* 6, 369.
[24] *WA* 17 II, 11; 31 I, 419.

is a death with him who not only died, but rose and became the sin of sin, the hell of hell, and the death of death.[25] The new life of the Christian is beyond himself; it is the life of the Spirit. The Spirit alone forms the link between the spiritual use of the law and the gospel.[26] God's love, his proper work, makes it possible for man to die and so to "live in Christ."

This twofold aspect connects the Christian sacrifice with baptism.[27] His priesthood rests on his baptism, and his baptism in turn is realized by his sacrifice—the death of the old Adam and the daily birth of the new man. Worship is the means by which the Spirit continues this fellowship and conformity with Christ.

Thus sacrifice cannot be identified with any particular liturgical act, not even with the prayers. It rests on the believer's fellowship with Christ and as such it is hidden.[28] It is related to that inner righteousness which may be expressed in externals, yet can never be deduced from them. For good works are always ambiguous; they may or may not flow from faith in God. While the sacrifice of the Christian priesthood may be realized in certain liturgical acts, it cannot be identified with them.

The Sacrifice of Praise and Thanksgiving

The priestly sacrifice of the believer is primarily one of praise and thanksgiving. This Luther often called the only true wor-

[25] *WA* 57, 129.

[26] *WA* 31 I, 419, 249; 57, 221 (Hb); Cf. R. Prenter, *Spiritus Creator*, pp. 13ff, 219ff.

[27] See e.g. *WA* 30 I, 220f, 382f; R. Josefson, *Luther on Baptism* (Hongkong: 1952), pp. 27ff, 61ff, 190f.

[28] In Luther's view the sacrificial moment may be connected only with the use by faith of the work of God. This is the reason why worship as the work of God used in faith may be defined as sacrifice, a sacrifice of thanksgiving by which the believer publicly confesses the benefits of God. Faith as worship implies that this sacrifice of faith would permeate all of worship. This confirms P. Brunner's description of the sacramental and sacrificial elements in worship as permeating each other.

ship.[29] For thanksgiving is man's response to the mercy of God. And within the church service it is conditioned by God's prior coming in Word and sacrament.[30] The rhythm of worship leads from the reception of the means of grace to thanksgiving and prayer, from the gift of God to the faith of the recipient. These two components cannot be separated, for worship cannot be without faith. An faith is at the heart of praise and thanksgiving.

Since God is the only one who can truly "give," man can render nothing but praise. And praise is the only service that is expected of him.[31] The cause is God's mercy and our sacrifice of praise and thanksgiving the result, or as Luther says in a sermon on the ten lepers (Luke 17:11-19):[32] "True worship is to turn back and with a loud voice glorify the Lord. This is the greatest work in heaven and on earth, indeed the only one that we may give to God, for he needs no other and accepts nothing from us but love and praise. To 'turn back' is to return to God the grace and goods we received of him, not to keep or grasp them, not to boast or demand credit from them, not to despise others or be pleased with ourselves for them, but to give all the glory to him who gave them and to suffer willingly if he should take them again and even then to love and praise him. Oh, how few they are who so 'turn back' indeed—hardly one in ten."

Thus, as a "turning back," man's gratitude includes the denial of himself and of his work. Renouncing his own glory he surrenders it to God where it belongs.[33] The rendering of thanks keeps him from crediting his physical or spiritual blessings to his own ability or to human instruments. Here again we note the

[29] *WA* 10 I, 2, 80; 49, 549 (print); 31 I, 251.
[30] *WA* 6, 526; 12, 565; 49, 588 (print); 42, 499.
[31] *WA* 10 I, 1, 714; 6, 218; 31 I, 251, 76; 6, 526.
[32] *WA* 8, 378-379.
[33] *WA* 10 I, 1, 715.

basic role faith in the Creator plays in Luther's theology of worship.[34]

His exposition of the Magnificat expresses beautifully the connection between the works of God and man's thanksgiving. To "sing praises" (to magnify) is interpreted as to "make great." Since our song praises his works, it acknowledges God as the Almighty who has all things in his hands.[35] This gives a personal facet to our song of praise, for God is indeed "great" in himself. He rules the world even without the praises of man. But it is when he becomes great "in us," in our "thoughts and feelings," that this rule becomes good news to us, for then it enters our own inner life.[36]

Luther also said that God becomes God by receiving the thanks of men. By giving thanks we let the gifts of God touch our hearts and so experience him as the one he really is.[37] As by our praise he becomes "our God," our idolatries are swept away and we are led thankfully to confess him as the great Giver of every good and perfect gift.[38]

The Reformer gives to our act of thanksgiving a twofold implication. As we praise and acknowledge the works of God, we renounce our own works and every claim that is based on them. We live of and under the works of God. This utter renunciation of work righteousness constitutes the Christian's sacrifice of praise and thanksgiving. To ask credit for our work is to rob God of the praise that our lips express, for it is possible for the very praise of man to become a work by which he tries to win his own right-

[34] Cf. the psalm verses often quoted by Luther: Psalm 50:12-14 (for example, *WA* 8, 378). See R. Bring, *On the Lutheran Concept*, p. 37ff.
[35] *WA* 7, 553, 545, 554.
[36] *WA* 7, 554; 30 II, 603.
[37] *WA* 30 II, 602-603.
[38] *WA* 31 I, 235. Cf. 16, 444 (Roerer and Aurifaber).

eousness. Man may remain godless in his "religion." While his worship may be perfectly correct, humanly speaking, he may still seek his own and deny God the honor that is due him.[39] The "religious," far from thanking God by their sacrifice, expect him to thank them for their acts of devotion.[40]

Man cannot glorify God without sacrificing himself, the old man, so often represented by his reason.[41] His offering of praise is hidden under the old man being sacrificed. From his earliest works Luther stressed this two-sidedness of the sacrifice of praise.

We note especially two complementary ideas: the praise of God and the accusation of self *(laus dei* and *accusatio sui);* and the confession of praise and the confession of sin *(confessio laudis* and *confessio peccati).*

In his early lectures on the Psalms Luther pointed out that man must renounce his own glory in order to glorify God.[42] The proud, by failing to confess God's goodness, robs him of his honor. But the humble believer will confess his sins as he praises God. In his need, the works of God become great to him.[43]

This connection between the confession of praise and that of sin may indeed be broken, and that in a twofold way. The sinner can despair over his sin. He examines himself without lifting his eyes to God and accepting his gifts. Such a man cannot praise God. He is lost, because even in the confession of his sins he clings to himself and thinks that he ought to effect rather than accept his righteousness.[44] Or else he presumes to praise God

[39] See especially *WA* 56, 356. E. Schott, *op. cit.*, p. 20ff.
[40] *WA* 30 [I], 3; 7, 567.
[41] *WA* 40 [I], 370.
[42] *WA* 3, 191, 292, 648; 4, 241.
[43] *WA* 1, 447. R. Josefson, *Oedmjukhet och tro* (Stockholm: 1939), p. 45ff; Otto Guehloff, *Gebieten und Schaffen Gottes in Luthers Auslegung des ersten Gebotes* (Goettingen: 1939), p. 14ff.
[44] *WA* 4, 238.

without condemning himself. But as long as he continues in his sin, his song remains an empty show.[45]

It is when man by faith receives the love of God that he is led from the confession of sin to the confession of praise.[46] By confessing his sins, he praises God, for he admits God's justice in his judgment.[47] In the depth of repentance, the Holy Spirit is at hand and teaches him the art of praising God.[48] In this sense, thanksgiving is in itself a sacrifice. And it is only the believer who can rightly bring the sacrifice of praise and confession.[49]

This connection between the confession of sin and the sacrifice of praise rests on the uneasy equation of gospel and law. Here man stands before the hidden God whom he cannot search. Only by faith can he receive the Holy Spirit who is the first fruits of the new creation and who teaches him how to sing praises unto God.[50] For the Holy Spirit inspires faith in God who grants life to those who were killed by the law and raises the lowly through the gospel.[51] Luther therefore called the hymn of praise "happy suffering and the proper work of God."[52] It is an act of receiving rather than giving on the part of man. The song of praise is a mark of heavenly life and joins the church militant with the church triumphant in heaven.[53] Only in hell, where there is no salvation, is the song of praise not heard.[54] Thus the priestly sacrifice of praise must be seen and interpreted on the basis of the work of God, for God acts through law and gospel, wrath and love. Man's confession and praise imply that he has shared the work of God. That explains why Luther called the sermon

[45] *WA* 4, 238. [46] *WA* 56, 268; 56, 290.
[47] *WA* 3, 173, 191, and 512; 56, 214 and 215.
[48] See Prenter, *op. cit.*, p. 5ff, on *odium sui—accusatio sui.*
[49] *WA* 3, 287. [50] *WA* 31 I, 406.
[51] *WA* 7, 546; 18, 633; 40 II, 458. [52] *WA* 7, 550.
[53] *WA* 6, 218. [54] *WA* 1, 162 (exposition of Ps. 6:5).

a sacrifice of praise, for it is the task of the ministry to crucify the old man and raise the new man to the glory of God.

"Here [I Peter 2:5] he refers to the office of preaching which is the true office of sacrifice [Ps. 50:23] . . . for by preaching the grace of God is praised, and that is to offer praise and thanksgiving, even as St. Paul boasts in Romans 16 [15:16?] of sanctifying or offering the gospel."[55] "Therefore our task is simply to praise and thank him, first, by receiving and believing in our hearts that from him are all things and that he is our God; and secondly by coming out with it and freely confessing it with our mouths before the world, preaching, praising, lauding, and thanking. This is the only true worship, the true priestly service, and the sacrifice, beloved and acceptable, as says St. Peter in I Peter 2 [vs.5]."[56] "He who thus preaches, teaches, and expounds, stabs the calf, the fleshly mind, and kills the old Adam. . . . The true priesthood is carried on where we offer the wicked knave, the lazy old donkey, to God."[57]

The total work which the church performs through the means of grace is only the sacrifice of the New Covenant—the priestly office performed by all those who by faith in Christ mortify the old Adam. And the worship of the church is an act of thanksgiving through the sacrifice of praise of the new man. However this must not be understood to mean that the proclamation of the Word and the administration of the sacraments have been instituted by the believers. Faith as an offering of praise does not create worship. It accepts it through the gospel. By receiving the work of God in faith, the church is confessing the mercy of God.[58] The believers are priests "for the world." And the crucifixion of the old man takes place as the gospel in the world meets

[55] *WA* 17 II, 8.
[56] *WA* 31 I, 251. Cf. also 12, 381ff; 31 I, 169.
[57] *WA* 12, 308.
[58] *WA* 30 I, 187; 10 I, 1, 140.

with opposition, contempt, and persecution.[59] This leads to a testing of our faith, and so man in his total life becomes an offering of praise unto the Lord.

In the course of church history, the Lord's Supper has been referred to as the sacrament of thanksgiving. What did Luther have to say about the idea of the Lord's Supper as a "Eucharist"? In his *Vermahnung zum Sakrament* (1530) he points out the connection between thank offering and faith and criticizes the Roman mass as a *Werkopfer* (work offering).[60] He rejects the view which would make a sacrifice of the Sacrament itself, that is, as a liturgical act. In itself it is a gift from God and nothing else. But the command of Christ, "this do in remembrance of me," belongs to the celebration of the Sacrament, for the Sacrament is to be celebrated with thanksgiving, with a faith which lauds and extols the Lord, but does not presume to offer anything. The very nature of the Sacrament as a gift of the merciful God fills the heart with nothing but gratitude.[61]

But Luther is no way confined the idea of thank offering to the Sacrament.[62] Nor did he, by the use of this idea, yield an inch from his earlier condemnation of the theology of sacrifice.[63] That the Sacrament is a thank offering means neither more nor less than that it must be observed in faith.

In *Von Anbeten des Sakraments* (On the Adoration of the Sacrament) Luther dealt with the adoration of the Sacrament. As he explains it, adoration is as little bound to the Sacrament as is thanksgiving. The God who wants to be worshiped in spirit and in truth (John 4:23) is bound to no specific localities or

[59] *WA* 8, 379.
[60] *WA* 30 II, 614 and 610.
[61] *WA* 6, 218, 231; 30 II, 603.
[62] See *WA* 3, 283; 6, 369.
[63] This was supposed to be the case by W. Thomas in "Das eucharistische Opfer nach dem lutherischen Bekenntnis," in *Deo omnia unum*, p. 289f.

occasions.[64] Christ is in the Sacrament not to be revered but to be received in faith.[65] This reception is the true worship in spirit and truth whether or not the worshiper faithfully performed every act of devotion. These acts of devotion may indeed express his gratitude to God.[66] But in that case it ceases to be a special work. Adoration and faith become one and the same act.[67] Luther was therefore quite ready to preserve the traditional liturgical forms of thanksgiving and adoration as long as they implied only the idea of thanksgiving and not that of the sacrifice of the mass.[68] He gladly accepted the hymns of the Middle Ages in the Reformed worship of praise, and enriched the liturgical thank offering through chorales of his own. But above all he prized the hymns of Scripture. The Holy Spirit was for him the greatest poet and singer of praise to the Lord.[69]

The Sacrifice of Prayer

Luther saw the sacrifice of praise (*sacrificium laudis*) to be in closest relation to the sacrifice of prayer *(sacrificium orationis)*. In the former we thank God for benefits received, in the latter we solicit further gifts from him.[70] Both sacrifices are based on faith. Our prayer rests on the experience of grace received. It includes gratitude for past mercies with confidence in the future. It is properly a form of thanksgiving.[71]

Both the sacrifice of praise and that of prayer belong within the celebration of the mass. But Luther denounced the medieval assumption which held prayers said at mass to be more effective than others. "Private" masses especially had been celebrated with

[64] *WA* 11, 444-445.
[65] *WA* 11, 447, 448.
[66] *WA* 11, 448, 449.
[67] *WA* 11, 446.
[68] *WA* 30 II, 614. Cf. 12, 206f.
[69] *WA* 31 I, 393.
[70] *WA* 30 II, 622.
[71] *WA* 10 I, 2, 183, 61.

the sole purpose of reinforcing the petitions of the faithful.[72] This had tended to divorce the sacrifice of prayer from that of praise and thanksgiving and to rob the prayers of their most important element: surrender to the will of God and confidence in his mercy.[73]

Contrariwise it was stressed by Luther that the Christian prays solely because of God's command and his promise to hear our prayers. His prayer is not a stab in the dark, nor a search for the unknown, but an exercise of faith, obedience, and hope, based on the mercy and works of God.[74] Thus prayer is not a work of merit nor is God's response a reward of our aspiration.[75] Without faith, man's most fervent devotions are an uncertain venture and amount to tempting God.[76] It is faith in God's command and his promises that will cleanse our prayer from selfish demands and wishes. It is enough for us to know that God wants to be asked and is right at hand as we bend our knees. And if he hears our prayers, we may conclude, not that our devotions were rewarded, but that he is fulfilling his promise.[77] Thus prayer, far from being man's long-distance call to God, is simply the exercise of faith in his promises which cannot fail.[78]

God's promise is that he will hear our prayers. This promise implies the remission of sins, for nothing entitles us to be heard except the mercy of God in Christ. Therefore we can pray only in the confidence that God is willing to overlook our sins.[79] This is what Luther meant by saying that under the New Covenant our prayer is always directed to Christ.[80]

[72] *WA* 6, 522; 30 II, 623. This medieval development is according to L. Fendt (*op. cit.*, p. 22f.) the "objectivation" of the mass as distinguished from the praise and thanksgiving of the early Christian Supper.
[73] *WA* 6, 522; 30 II, 623. [74] *WA* 30 I, 193, 195, 396; 32, 489; 6, 232.
[75] *WA* 2, 175. [76] *WA* 30 I, 195. [77] *WA* 2, 175.
[78] *WA* 30 I, 196. [79] *WA* 2, 176. [80] *WA* 9, 230.

The sacrifice of prayer, like that of praise, is an act of self-denial and commitment to Christ, for all prayers, the ones in the mass included, are addressed to God in the name of Christ.[81] It is the prayer "in the name of Jesus," "for the sake of Christ" or "through Christ" which accepts the promise and approaches God by faith. Such prayer recalls one who is great before God and for whose sake God is ready to forgive our sins and hear our petitions.[82] Christ is the altar upon which the one who prays is sacrificed and from which his petitions ascend to God.[83] Thus prayer and praise blend into one. To pray through Christ means to make God great *(magnificare),* to appropriate all his benefits, and so to laud and confess him as our Saviour.

Yet prayer is not a device for mastering God or for prescribing how he should help in a given need. On the contrary, to pray in faith means to deny oneself and one's own desires in favor of God's will and rule. The man who prays need do no more than to bring his wants before God, and the Lord will respond as will be best.[84] "Thy will be done" should be the lodestar of every prayer. Human reason would like to prescribe a course of action for the Lord, but faith is content to submit to God's more perfect will.[85] Luther even spoke of prayer as a resignation by the believer to hell *(resignatio ad infernum),*[86] for the believer will trust in the fulfilment of his prayer, even though God should grant, not what he wants, but what he needs.[87]

Luther therefore said that every prayer is heard. Only the unbeliever complains of petitions that went unheard. He has failed to deny his selfish wishes in the first place, and wrongly lets his

[81] *WA* 6, 368.
[82] *WA* 10 I, 2, 183; 7, 518; 11, 445.
[83] *WA* 10 I, 2, 184; 3, 646. [84] *WA* 51, 606; 2, 177.
[85] *WA* 6, 368; 19, 96. [86] *WA* 9, 140. [87] *WA* 6, 232.

gratitude depend on the satisfaction of what he demanded.[88] But the believer, whose prayer springs from total self-surrender, accepts God's response as best whichever it may be.[89] Faith is waiting for the works of God. Prayer and faith are therefore one. Faith implies prayer.[90] And faith like that insures the proper reception of the mass.[91]

All this Luther had learned from the Lord's Prayer. And he hoped that this prayer—"the greatest martyr on earth"[92]—would teach the church again how to pray.[93] He looked upon it as the prayer of the communion of saints,[94] for the Saviour had given it to the disciples as a group. So today it should deliver the believer from loneliness, for he is within the congregation.

Luther wrote several expositions of the Lord's Prayer and urged that it be used with the heart, and not with the lips alone.[95] While he condemned the mechanical repetition of stated prayers, he did not reject the faithful use of the Lord's own prayer or of the Psalms.[96] In biblical prayers he found a school for faith.

[88] God fulfils prayers differently from what we wish and imagine because he is hidden. In his Lectures on Romans Luther goes so far as to say that it is a good sign when God does not hear our prayers (*WA* 57, 375), for we must be made poor and needy before he will take mercy on us. Cf. also the quotations cited by O. Dittrich (*op. cit.*, p. 88f). Walther von Loewenich finds in this problem the whole theology of the cross in a nutshell.

[89] *WA* 18, 519. Cf. S. Lerfeldt, *Den kristnes kamp*, p. 169.

[90] *WA* 8, 360; 17 II, 76; 18, 495, 519.

[91] *WA* 6, 236, 238. [92] *WA* 38, 364. [93] *WA* 10 II, 376.

[94] *WA* 2, 86, 114; 6, 12. [95] *WA* 2, 82.

[96] In Luther's *Betbuechlein* (Prayer Booklet) from 1522 (*WA* 10 II, 375ff) one finds only stated prayers out of the tradition of the church (The Ten Commandments, the Creed, the Hail Mary, a few psalms and the Epistle to Titus). In 38, 364 Luther says of himself: "To this day I suck on the Lord's Prayer like a child" and enumerates the same prayers as above. In 50, 641 he names the Word of God and the Catechism as prayers. He was wont to think of the Word as being prayed. Thus he says in *Von Ordnung Gottesdiensts* (12, 35): "The Christian congregation should never come together, unless the Word of God is preached and prayed."

A man has to pass through this school and be firm in the faith before he can offer "free prayers."[97] And the Lord's Prayer remains the standard for them.[98] An example of the standard is the order of its petitions. The first petition clears the second from human ideas of the kingdom. The third relegates the benefits sought in the last four to their proper place.[99] And the fourth serves to justify all other prayers for gifts material and earthly.[100]

Prayer as a sacrifice implies not only the self-denial and crucifixion of the old man within us, but also a priestly service with and for others. By renouncing his selfish desires, the believer will be ready to intercede for others.[1] Intercession was for Luther the most important part of liturgical prayer.[2]

The communion of saints is, among other things, a fellowship of prayer. God's command points us to our fellow, also in prayer.[3] Here awakens the new life, for the Word has splendid promises for the common prayer of the church. It is the foremost weapon against the devil, and the latter tries to hinder it in every way.[4]

[97] *WA* 2, 85.

[98] *WA* 2, 82; 6, 11.

[99] *WA* 6, 21, 22.

[100] In connection with the sixth petition of the Lord's Prayer, Luther recalled the litany which he re-introduced in Wittenberg in 1529 in response to the dangers from the Turks. See the text of his German and Latin Litany in 30 III, 29ff. For Luther's emphasis on intercession during the Turkish Wars, see Richard Lind, *Luthers Stellung zum Kreutz- und Tuerkenkrieg* (Giessen: 1940), p. 56ff.

Since the Lord's Prayer seemed to include every petition that is necessary, Luther was content to include in the German Mass a paraphrase of it. He felt that all prayers should be patterned along the lines of the Lord's Prayer and saw no need to replace the prayers of the Canon Missae by prayers other than the Lord's Prayer paraphrased. The insertion of a paraphrase instead of the original text may have been motivated by the desire to prevent a mechanical repetition of the well-known text. At any rate it agrees with his own advice for the practice of prayer. Every prayer is basically a meditation on the "Our Father." Thus the Lord's Prayer was made to dominate public as well as private devotions. Cf. G. Kappner, *op. cit.,* p. 42.

[1] *WA* 12, 186f.

[2] *WA* 6, 237.

[3] *WA* 6, 242.

[4] *WA* 49, 594; 6, 232, 239.

Intercessory prayer is a mark of the church. Enthusiasts do not practice it because they are concerned only with their own salvation. Nor did the medieval fraternities. To Luther their whole prayer-life was selfish and egotistical.[5] But in the communion of saints, the believers bear each other's burdens in prayer. Indeed, they bring the burdens of all the world, of believers and unbelievers, good and bad, friend and foe, before the throne of God.[6] As the disciples of Christ, they invoke the blessing of God on every state and condition of man.

Thus they confess both their solidarity with all mankind and the givenness of their righteousness. This righteousness, since it is Christ's, they cannot accept as their own, nor hope to keep it except as they pass it on to others.[7] And as the church prays for the world, it joins in the priesthood of him who sits at the right hand of God and intercedes for us.[8]

The Material Sacrifice in the Calling

A third form of sacrifice consists of the material offerings by which Christians return their earthly gifts to the Lord. Luther recalled especially the offertory act in the early church.[9] Here the first fruits were presented at the altar to show that all the gifts of the earth are of God. God did not demand these gifts for himself. The gifts deposited at the altar were ultimately given to the poor and needy.[10] Luther regretted the discontinuance of this custom. In his day, Christian stewardship no longer benefited the needy, but was exclusively directed towards the upkeep of monas-

[5] *WA* 2, 114.
[6] *WA* 10 I, 1, 435, 436; 6, 375, 522. Cf. K. Thieme, *Die sittliche Triebkraft des Glaubens* (Leipzig: 1895), p. 57f, and the Luther passages quoted there.
[7] *WA* 2, 86, 148; 6, 242.
[8] *WA* 6, 370.
[9] *WA* 1, 446; 2, 747; 6, 365ff, 524; 30 II, 294. Cf. 18, 104.
[10] *WA* 6, 366.

teries and the erection of churches. He had no quarrel with the use of these funds for the church's works of mercy.[11] But he objected to monks depending on charity simply because they disdained to enter a secular calling. By the same token he criticized the practice of votive masses and stressed the difference between true sacrifice and the false sense of security which people derived from their payment for special masses.[12]

On the other hand, he found a truly Christian idea of sacrifice expressed in the collect, in the offertory, and in its elevation.[13] These, he thought, were the original prayers over the gifts collected, as the latter were set apart for the poor.[14] Nevertheless he made no move towards reviving the ancient custom of an offering within the service, but suggested instead that a spiritual sacrifice should take the place of the material. Here we should offer up "ourselves and all that we have."[15]

Had he, in spite of the early Christian precedent, surrendered every thought of connecting worship and material sacrifice (stewardship)? In answering this question, it must be noted that Luther recognized an intimate relation between worship and its evidence in works of Christian love. These works are born and nourished by the "sacrament of love." The communion of saints exists not only in receiving the gifts of God, but in the sacrifice of love which believers bring for each other.[16] Baptism is realized

[11] *WA* 6, 366.

[12] *WA* 6, 521.

[13] *WA* 6, 366. This distinction between the elevation in the offertory and the one in connection with the Words of Institution is quite proper. The theological meaning of the elevation at these points is indeed totally different. See J. A. Jungmann, *Missarum Sollemnia* (Wien: 1949), in the index under "Erhebung als Darbringungsritus."

[14] Provisionally he did therefore tolerate these prayers, as long as they were only connected with the unconsecrated gifts (*WA* 6, 524). But in *Vom Greuel der Stillmesse* (1525), Luther says that the prayers before the consecration expressed an idea of sacrifice that could not be reconciled with *Darbringungsopfer* (material sacrifice). See above p. 54ff.

[15] *WA* 6, 368.

[16] *WA* 2, 745; 6, 519; 30 II, 617.

as the old Adam is drowned and destroyed in the tasks, trials, and sacrifices of daily life. Worship has its immediate bearing on the Christian's attitude in the hurly-burly of the workaday world.[17] And we see again the familiar features of Luther's picture of sacrifice—the death of the old and the rising of the new man—in his thoughts on the effect of our worship on daily life, though he started more often from the idea of the communion of saints than from that of sacrifice.[18]

In the course of his controversies with the papists and later with the Enthusiasts, Luther allowed this whole thought to recede to the background[19] although it was never abandoned completely. But ultimately he developed it along the lines of his idea of "calling." While he no longer employed the term of "sacrifice" in this context, the idea is clearly implied in his theology of the calling.

Gustaf Wingren has been able to show the relation between Luther's view of the calling and the death of the old and life of the new man. Man's daily calling is the place where the old man is crucified. With this presentation, Wingren has taught us to see Luther's theology of the cross from a new angle.[20]

The Christian brings his sacrifice as he renders the obedience, offers the service, and proves the love which his work and calling require of him. The old man dies as he spends himself for his

[17] *WA* 2, 734, 735, 736; 50, 643. See also C. Stange, *Studien zur Theologie Luthers* (Guetersloh: 1928), I, p. 384f.

[18] Cf. H. Olsson, *Grundproblemet i Luthers socialetik,* where the author points out that the Christian priesthood implies a surrender of all that is our own for the neighbor, and so a sacrifice of our body in the service of neighborly love.

[19] This does not imply, as Y. Brilioth too confirms (*op. cit.,* p. 98), that the whole thought had disappeared.

[20] G. Wingren (*Luther on Vocation,* p. 50ff) shows the connection between the Christian's cross and his calling, an idea that Karl Eger, *Die Anschauungen Luthers vom Beruf* (Giessen: 1900) and Paul H. Schifferdecker, *Der Berufsgedanke bei Luther* (Heidelberg: 1932) had failed to detect.

fellow-men. But in this surrender of self, he is joined to Christ and obtains a new life.[21] The work of the Christian in his calling becomes a function of his priesthood, his bodily sacrifice.[22] His work in the calling is a work of faith, the worship of the kingdom of the world.

And so the idea of the calling tends to expand the whole meaning of worship. Worship is not confined to pious exercises in the sanctuary but includes the whole of Christian life in service and self-surrender to the needs of the world. Our stewardship and offering of material gifts retain their close relation to the liturgy. But they are vastly more than a liturgical act. The latter might be a mere fragment, a work of merit, brought forward to obtain the grace of God. But true bodily sacrifice is a total, continued giving of self which includes both faith and action.[23]

The adjective "spiritual" implies the role of faith in our sacrifice. Even material sacrifices become "spiritual" when rendered to God in faith. For faith directs us to devote our gifts to the

[21] *WA* 7, 66.

[22] In his book *Den korsfaeste Skaparen* (Stockholm: 1952), Torgny Bohlin has proved that the social problems in Luther's ethics must also be understood from the reality of the resurrection which causes the Christian to live his life within the orders of creation in the confidence that all of creation has been comprehended in the victory of resurrection (especially p. 307ff). This interpretation throws light on the role of the priesthood of all believers in this connection (p. 376ff). The cross in one's calling (death) and the resurrection form a *communicatio,* which is characteristic of Luther and which fails to receive full justice in Wingren's above-named book. Wingren himself realized this lack and implied a certain correction in his book *Predikan* (p. 307, especially footnote 22).

[23] My relation to the neighbor (in office or service) implies the death of the self. By serving another my own ego dies. In his table talks, Luther said about the plague which was then raging in Wittenberg (*WA* TR 4, 511): "If you have a wife, child, brother, sister, or neighbor, stay and help. We owe a death to one another." Likewise in the pamphlet *Ob man vor dem Sterben fliehen moege* (Whether it is permissible to flee death) (1527), the main thought is that those in an office dare not leave their neighbors behind (see especially *WA* 23, 341ff).

neighbor's good, rather than to our own. As a matter of fact, the sacrifices which we give to the neighbor are given to God, for Christ is with us here on earth. He is the one who both gives and receives.[24] By this relation to him, our sacrifices are spiritual indeed.

[24] *WA* 23, 363; 14, 613 (V); 6, 7, 212, 227; 8, 466, 626; 12, 337; 36, 353, 361, etc.

8

Faith (Freedom) and Love (Order) in Worship

In the last two chapters the ceremonies of the church (the liturgical forms) were left aside. What have they to do with worship as the work of faith? The answer to this question will be found in this discussion of the theological significance of liturgical forms from the twofold viewpoint of faith and love, or of freedom and order.

Order in Freedom

Luther defines the Christian faith as freedom and the Christian as a man set free.[1] Faith implies liberty in all the works of man, of the law, and therewith of liturgical forms too.[2] The believer need not give anything to God, but lives by the gifts he receives from him.[3] His freedom is based on God's coming to him and on his own conformity with Christ.[4] As a recipient of the "alien

[1] *WA* 7, 49. Swedish scholars have devoted several monographs to the problem of Christian freedom, as for example Arvid Runestam, *Den Kristliga friheten hos Luther och Melanchton* (Stockholm: 1917), and *Viljans frihet och den kristliga friheten* (Uppsala: 1921); H. Olsson, *Grundproblemet i Luthers socialetik*, I; and G. Wingren, *Luther on Vocation.* But most of these works have remained unknown because of language limitations, as Wilhelm Maurer's important study, *Von der Freiheit eines Christenmenschen* (Goettingen: 1949), shows.

[2] Runestam, *Den Kristliga friheten*, p. 107ff.

[3] *WA* 7, 50.

[4] *WA* 7, 56. Maurer (*op. cit.*, pp. 36ff, 57) tries to prove that Luther's thought of a "happy interchange" between the believer and Christ derives not from medieval mysticism but from the idea of the mystery (*Mysterientheologie*) of the early church.

righteousness" of Christ, he needs no works or merits to be justified,[5] let alone the ceremonies of the church.[6]

However, this liberty must not be seen as a liberty from God or from his works. Only as man partakes in Christ and in his works can he be free. His liberty is through, not from the gospel,[7] and commensurate to his bondage under the same.[8]

But in the faith he is independent of human forms and rites, of holy places, seasons, vestments, and all the like. The gospel and faith are his worship.[9] Liturgical forms and rites cannot affect his conscience, for his faith does not rest on outward things. It is an inward trust in the redeeming work of Christ.

Of course, this applies only to the rites introduced by men. Man-made orders of service must never be held essential for salvation, for in matters of the kingdom men are apt to err.[10] Yet freedom from man-made laws does not imply freedom from Christ. Externals instituted by the Lord must not be equated with those that were added later. We may be free from man-made forms but we are bound to those instituted by Christ. We cannot be free from the "external" Word of the gospel, nor from the external things of the sacraments.[11] This emphasis steered Lu-

[5] The christological basis of Christian freedom lies in this connection between "alien righteousness" and Christian liberty. Olsson saw this fact more clearly than did Runestam.

[6] *WA* 7, 50-52; 40 I, 161, 673; 40 II, 454; 7, 70.

[7] This is the basis of *De Servo Arbitrio*, where the will in bondage corresponds to the view of freedom as presented above. Cf. Wingren, *Luther on Vocation*, pp. 17ff, 93ff, and Runestam, *Viljans frihet*, p. 38f, 42ff.

[8] Runestam, *Den Kristliga friheten*, p. 112ff.

[9] *WA* 10 I, 1, 39.

[10] *WA* 10 I, 2, 79; 10 II, 86.

[11] While free from every law, the Christian service is bound to the "ceremonies" instituted by God, that is, the means of grace; cf. Th. Knolle, *op. cit.*, p. 8ff, 11ff. *Luthers Reform der Abendmahlsfeier*, p. 91; P. Brunner, p. 16ff. P. Flemming's thesis "that the ideal service is completely unliturgical" and that "the characteristic of the ideal Lutheran service is liturgical formlessness" does not agree with Luther (*op. cit.*, pp. 47, 58).

ther's reform of worship between the Scylla and Charybdis of legalism and spiritualism.

To him, both papists and Enthusiasts were enemies of Christian liberty. Both meant to replace faith with human rites. The pope had bound the conscience of men to certain works. Fasts and private confession, sacred times and places had been made essential for the Christian faith. By their mere performance, these works were supposed to warrant the mercy of God. And so the pope had intruded into the sphere of almighty God and presumed to bind or loose the consciences of men.[12] Some of these rites were wrong in themselves and had to be swept away, like the countless acts of consecration which did not accord with the Word of God.[13] Others might be retained or removed, according to the verdict of the individual conscience. But even this freedom the pope was unwilling to grant.

The Enthusiasts, on the other hand, made a law of that evangelical freedom which Luther proclaimed.[14] Whatever the pope had commanded for salvation, they meant to prohibit. They failed to see that man is justified neither by the performance nor by the neglect of certain rites. They tyrannized the conscience of men as much as the pope and were as slow to grant freedom in the use of liturgical forms.

The freedom which Luther stressed had to do with man's position before God. He did not dispute the importance of works,

[12] *WA* 18, 112. J. Heckel rightly points out that Luther in the struggle over indulgences raised a basic question of canon law, namely, whether the highest authority in the church on earth should have the right of effectively remitting works of penance in the world to come, that is, to legislate for the kingdom of Christ. Roman tradition answered in the affirmative, while Luther denied it.

[13] *WA* 50, 644: "Thus he [the devil] through the popes and papists caused water, salt, herbs, candles, bells, pictures, Agnus Dei, chasubles, pates, fingers, and hands to be dedicated or consecrated. Who can tell it all?"

[14] *WA* 18, 11; 7, 69, 70.

ceremonial or otherwise, for the outward life of man.[15] But he felt that only those who are inwardly free of forms and rites are able to use them rightly.[16] There is no harm in liturgical forms, unless they are made an essential tool to get to heaven. Luther condemned their abuse, but not their proper use in faith.[17]

This world needs order and form.[18] And so does our worship here. It must be appointed for certain days and times. It cannot be held without liturgical forms, for while "the inner man is free and subject to none," the "outer man is bound and subject to all." [19] The man who before God is passive and can only receive, is active towards his fellow-men. Before the Lord he stands alone, a single person, but in his outward life he is related to countless others.[20] This relation is one of loving service, for he becomes a channel through whom the love he received from God flows on to his neighbors.[21]

It is this love for his fellow-men that prompted Luther's conservative approach to the question of liturgical reform. The believer indeed is free of stated forms of worship. He worships in

[15] *WA* 7, 70.

[16] Occasionally Luther's humor finds expression in his description of Christian liberty, as for example *WA* 26, 570: "For thank goodness, we have strong enough skulls to wear a tonsure, our stomachs and bellies are healthy enough to fast and eat and digest fish on Friday and Saturday, especially since they allow us to drink good wine with it (doubtless for added chastisement), and we have shoulders and bones strong enough to wear chasubles, surplices, and long robes. To sum it up, we are quite confident of keeping all their wonderful, great, and dear sanctity by our natural powers, without a special grace of the Holy Ghost, so that they need not to brag of their holy life too much. . . ."

[17] *WA* 7, 70; 10 I, 1, 28, 33f, especially 34.

[18] *WA* 5, 401. This comes also from the fact that life never stops; God is always active and spurs on the activity of man. See Wingren, *Luther on Vocation,* 78, 123ff.

[19] *WA* 7, 49.

[20] *WA* 32, 440; 19, 648. See Olsson, *Grundproblemet,* p. 202ff.

[21] *WA* 10 III, 3; 17 II, 74; A. Nygren, *Agape and Eros,* p. 733ff.

spirit and truth. Yet he submits to them, first because he himself is not a perfect Christian and needs to be trained in the faith, and second, in order to help his neighbor become a Christian and grow in the faith. "We appoint these orders not for those who are Christians already, for they don't need them. Nor do we need them. But they live for our sakes, that they might make us Christians, for they have their worship in the spirit." [22]

Thus Christian freedom implies no outright rejection of liturgical forms. The very fact that they are used for the good of the neighbor will keep us from expecting to gain merit and will be for us a discipline *(mortificatio)* and continued exercise of faith.[23]

Thus rites and ceremonies indeed form a training school of faith. To this extent, the pedagogical view is true to Luther. While ceremonies cannot create the faith, they can point to it.[24] They are the scaffolding needed for building the church, but must not be confused with the church itself.[25] They can serve to bring the immature (the young and simple folk) into the orbit of the Word and sacrament where faith is born. As long as man is "external," such outward orders will be needed for the sake of love, for love and order belong together.[26]

How then does the freedom implied in the Christian faith relate to the order demanded by love? Two answers must be given to this question: The two emphases are not contradictory, for both

[22] *WA* 19, 73. H. Olsson (*Grundproblemet,* pp. 119 and 126) establishes a parallel between the Christian's freedom from liturgical forms and his freedom from secular orders, which as a Christian he does not need either.

[23] A. Runestam (*Den Kristliga friheten,* p. 29) criticized Luther because in *De libertate* he allowed himself to be forced into a false premise by having to motivate the necessity of works. But Luther links works with "mortification" and with the exercise of faith even apart from the question of "good works." See Olsson, *Grundproblemet,* p. 114, n. 1.

[24] This is associated with the fact that ceremonies, like all other orders of the church, belong to the level of the law and are not the proper work of the church.

[25] *WA* 8, 378; 7, 72; 19, 113.

[26] *WA* 50, 649.

faith and love are constitutive for the Christian life. Secondly, the order of the two cannot be reversed. While faith leads to love, love does not necessarily lead to faith. Faith may become incarnate in the works of love. But love is not a preparation for faith. The inner life of man must necessarily find its expression in outward works.[27] But outward works can do nothing to establish his standing before God.

By the same token, rites and forms are natural and necessary for the outward life of man. They are useful as a means of discipline. But they cannot clear and justify us in the sight of God.[28] This place is reserved for the gospel—the work of God—and not the works of men.

Liturgical forms should therefore never be used except as a framework for the proclamation of the gospel. Jesus himself performed no works without interpreting them by his words. Liturgical forms without the preaching of the Word are like the outward (old) man without the inward (new) man of faith. It is only by the preaching of the gospel that the proper use of liturgical forms can be safeguarded.[29] The Word will prevent the worshipers from resting their faith on their own (liturgical) works, rather than on the work of God.

Man-made liturgies and ceremonies, orders and rites may

[27] See A. Runestam, "Introduktion i Luthers teologi med ledning av hans skrift om den kristna friheten" in *Efterskrift till M. Luther* (Stockholm: 1920), p. 37, and H. Olsson, *Grundproblemet*, p. 134ff where the connection between the *totus-homo* aspect and Christology is competently developed.

[28] *WA* 2, 82; 10 II, 36; 18, 66. Here Luther accuses the Enthusiasts of turning the order of grace upside down and trying to progress from the outward to the inward. Prenter, *op. cit.*, p. 248ff.

[29] *WA* 5, 401ff; 18, 768. The sacraments stand entirely on the side of the gospel, for their administration must always be linked with the proclamation of the work of Christ. Not even here is it lawful to speak of a spiritual power imparted through the act as such, apart from the proclamation of the gospel, for without this proclamation, the gifts of God are apt to be perverted to human efforts of presenting something to God.

therefore be used only in faith (in Christian liberty).[30] The believer can worship in forms both simple or ornate, as long as both will serve as a vehicle for his faith.[31]

The Pliancy of Order

We tried to show above that while the "inner man" is free from rites and laws, the "outer man" for the sake of love is bound to order and form. Christian liberty however also affects the exercise of love, for as the conscience cannot be bound to certain forms, neither can the external order. Love constrains us to worship according to stated forms, but it does not prescribe any particular set of rites.[32] The need for forms cannot be disputed, but their choice must be allowed to vary. To absolutize any single rite would be to jeopardize the freedom not only of Christian love, but also of Christian conscience.

The choice of forms is however not a matter of personal preference, but must depend on the need of our fellows. The liturgical choice of the "outer man," his decision for or against certain forms, should be dictated by the need of others.[33] In his outward relationships, man is bound to his surroundings, while in his conscience he is free from them. In concrete cases, therefore, he may act in seemingly contradictory ways, according to the demands of love.

Thus the form of worship need not be uniform or unchangeable. Neighborly love will call for many changes, even as a tree sprouts new blooms and fruits every year.[34] Luther's views on liturgical freedom reflect his broadmindedness and pliancy in

[30] *WA* 10 II, 37.
[31] *WA* 6, 380; 19, 113.
[32] *WA* 18, 764; 10 I, 2, 78.
[33] *WA* 6, 214; 26, 574; 10 I, 2, 78. The biblical references most often quoted in this connection are Matt. 17:25ff; Romans 14:1, and I Cor. 9:20f.
[34] *WA* 11, 442; 8, 609; 19, 113; 6, 214.

other matters of the Christian life. He was done with legalism on the street as well as in the sanctuary. Our neighbor's actual needs should dictate our liturgical decisions as well as our response in all other ethical questions.[35] Luther recalled the freedom of Christ, his apostles,[36] and of the Virgin Mary, who submitted to the requirements of the law although in conscience she was free of them.[37] It was their faith which had thus freed them, for in externals the Christian is bound to his neighbor only by love. But in his conscience he is free of every law.[38]

From this position, Luther could not but reject the liturgical legalism of the Roman church.[39] He had to break the bonds that chained the believers to the Roman canons of liturgical lore. His opponents sought to defend the hallowed traditions as those of the body of Christ, where the Spirit himself is at work. But Luther found the work of the Spirit not in laws and canons but in the freedom by which a Christian adapts himself to his neighbor's needs. Thus only could the door for God's continued intervention in the vicissitudes of history be kept ajar.[40] He rejected the ceremonial laws of the Roman church, not only because they held consciences in bondage, but also because they were contrary to the law of love.[41]

On the other hand and quite as decisively, he rejected the anti-

[35] One of the most important points that Wingren brought up for discussion in *Luther on Vocation* is the balance of flexibility and firmness in Luther's theology. He interprets the pliancy of Christian action as an expression of Luther's picture of God as one who is constantly creating anew.

[36] *WA* 10 I, 2, 175.

[37] *WA* 7, 66; 9, 656ff; 12, 421f. Luther liked to refer to Paul's flexible policy in the question of circumcision (he circumcised Timothy, but refused to circumcise Titus when the rite was made an issue). Like Paul, Luther wanted to be a Jew to the Jews, a Greek to the Greeks, and a Turk to the Turks; see 26, 581.

[38] *WA* 8, 609.

[39] *WA* 5, 405f; 40 I, 162.

[40] *WA* 10 I, 2, 175.

[41] *WA* 26, 573, 581.

liturgical biblicism of the Enthusiasts. They condemned every ecclesiastical tradition as such and would allow no liturgical form unless it could be traced right to the Bible. But Christ's example —as Luther was wont to point out—is not binding for us, except by express command. An attempt to imitate him in every detail would lead to nonsensical lengths and defeat itself.[42] In their own way, the Enthusiasts were as legalistic as the Romanists and as ignorant of the liberty implied in the Christian faith and demanded by Christian love.

Luther meant to follow a middle road *(Mittelbahn, via media)* between them and the papists.[43] He felt free to borrow from the right or the left,[44] for his picture of evangelical freedom lifted him far above the liturgical factions. The sectarianism of liturgical legalists was an offense to him,[45] for while the law will cause divisions, the gospel should bring about unity. Christ's kingdom is spiritual and does not depend on ceremonies and laws. These, though necessary, do not belong to his kingdom.[46] Luther's middle road is therefore not a spineless compromise, but the expression of Christian freedom.

Luther however distinguishes carefully between the so-called "ceremoniacs" (the papists and Enthusiasts) and the common people.[47] The latter clung to the traditional liturgical forms as tenaciously as the pope, but for different reasons. The ceremoniacs were smug and stubborn. But the people were conservative only because they were weak in faith.[48] Christian love demanded greater patience with them than with the self-righteous papists. After centuries of papist perversion, the people could not be expected to embrace the freedom of faith in a flash.[49]

[42] *WA* 18, 114f; 30 III, 526.
[43] *WA* 18, 122.
[44] *WA* 10 II, 24; 18, 112.
[45] *WA* 6, 353, 354; 10 I, 2, 176; 31 I, 210.
[46] *WA* 31 I, 233; 10 II, 202.
[47] *WA* 5, 404, 406; 7, 70f.
[48] *WA* 10 I, 2, 66.
[49] *WA* 6, 686.

Luther was well aware of this fact, and all his liturgical reforms betray his concern for the spiritual well-being of the weak in faith.[50] They needed a form of service which would provide for their edification without being bound to a single pattern.[51]

He warned the pastors against arbitrary changes of their own, for the liturgy must serve all who worship, so that no one may cling to the outward order, but that all may be helped to experience the freedom of faith.[52] This has to be preached from the pulpit and proven as well at the altar.

It is in this context that we must understand the liturgical options which are left to the officiant in the *Formula Missae*. They were meant, not to establish a liturgical dictatorship on the part of the parish pastor, but to allow some leeway for adapting the liturgy to changing circumstances. In things liturgical, as in other questions, Luther was stiff and unbending when it came to the defense of the faith, but pliant and flexible when the expression of Christian love was at stake; for love is needed in order to win for others the freedom of the Christian man.[53] And to receive our neighbors in their weakness is the proper priestly work toward them.[54]

[50] *WA* 26, 562; 12, 131.

[51] *WA* 10 I, 2, 67; Br. 3, 586. Allwohn's historical study offers many examples of Luther's considerate application of his principles in the actual reform of the service. To him, an absolute liturgical fixation was wrong in principle.

[52] *WA* 18, 419.

[53] *WA* 10 III, 7; 40 I, 212.

[54] Luther's attitude towards the so-called Wittenberg movement, which during his absence at the Wartburg effected radical liturgical changes, agrees fully with his thoughts as described above. Some scholars (notably, H. Barge, *Andreas Bodenstein von Karlstadt* [Leipzig: 1905], I, especially pp. 432-47, and following him N. Fransén, *Nya Studier* [Stockholm: 1941], p. 154) have claimed that Luther changed his views at this juncture and that his opposition to the Wittenberg movement had been influenced mostly by the concern of the authorities. Actually, however, his famous Invocavit sermons of 1522 (*WA* 10 III, 1-64) reflect what Luther had said earlier (especially in *Von*

Luther's "liturgical conservativism" must be seen against this background.[55] In his entire liturgical work, he remained within the tradition in which he had been raised. He limited himself to those liturgical forms which had come from the medieval church, and created no novel rites or appointments. This conservatism is hardly surprising. It springs from his concern for others. He would have contradicted his own conviction had he constructed a service from scratch and broken with a tradition of which, in spite of his bitter critique, he valued many features. He never thought of removing the Supper, as though it might encroach on the Word.[56] He gladly retained those parts of the mass that were free of the implication of sacrifice. But his love for the neighbor and his tolerance for inherited ceremonials stopped short at the sacrifice of the mass. Everything connected with it was removed without fail, for here faith was at stake.[57]

Thus he indeed reformed the mass, but never made an attempt to reconstruct it anew. This was not due to lack of interest or

beider Gestalt des Sakraments [1522], 10 II, 11-41 and *Von Menschenlehre zu meiden* [1522], 10 II, 11-14). The main points of Luther's rejection of the Wittenberg movement are the following: 1. The liturgical reform ought to proceed from the proclamation of the Word to external reforms, not vice versa (10 II, 37; 10 II, 17); 2. In every reform, the needs of the neighbor must be considered. Otherwise nothing but sectarianism results (10 III, 6, 8). It may be added that these thoughts are already in *Operationes in Psalmos* (1519-21) and in *De libertate christiana* (1520). W. Maurer has shown persuasively that Luther's popular presentation (as in the last-named pamphlet) grew out of his scholarly exegesis of the psalms. The same is true of the Invocavit sermons which are not a hasty compilation of novel thoughts, but rather constitute the application of insights developed much earlier. This disposes of the above-quoted allegation that Luther opposed the Wittenberg movement only in order to promote the efforts of the authorities to re-Catholicize the city.

[55] J. Gottschick, *op. cit.*, p. 69; Y. Brilioth, *op. cit.*, p. 110.

[56] The opposite view of G. Rietschel is an expression, not of Luther's view, but of modern Protestantism (*Lehrbuch der Liturgik*, I, p. 497). I did not see the second edition of Rietschel's work, newly edited by P. Graff (Goettingen 1951-2) until this book was in print. However there is nothing in this edition to correct my criticism, voiced here and above on pp. 18-25.

[57] *WA* 10 I, 2, 79.

knowledge, as has been charged so often. It stems directly from his teaching of righteousness by faith. Leonhardt Fendt has convincingly pointed out that a spanking new order of worship, "made in Wittenberg" and approved by Luther, would only have served to encourage a new brand of work righteousness and would have belied the freedom of faith which the Reformer had preached.[58]

The two orders which Luther published in the course of his liturgical reforms were made for the actual local congregation in Wittenberg. They were not meant to establish an ideal pattern for every Lutheran church to follow.[59] His liturgies were designed with due regard for the local custom and needs. And Luther never failed to declare that he meant to offer no more than an example, and certainly not a law.[60] Others, by following the same general principles, might arrive at very different orders in accordance with varying local traditions and needs.[61]

Thus the order of love precluded liturgical uniformity. Luther felt that a diversity in outward forms could easily be endured, as long as there was unity in the essentials. As a matter of fact, such diversity might keep people from assigning too much importance to the form of the service, and so from factionalism and sectarianism.[62] On the other hand and for the very same reason, Luther sought to avoid needless and senseless changes in the order of

[58] Fendt, *Der lutherische Gottesdienst,* p. 101ff.

[59] *WA* 12, 214; 19, 72.

[60] *WA* 12, 219; 19, 73.

[61] He was also skeptical about a church constitution worked out in detail at so early a date and therefore rejected the Hessian outline of a church constitution in a letter to Philip of Hesse (*WA* Br. 4, 157f). He thought that unwritten customs should first be established before being made binding by precepts and laws. The reverse he rejected, because it implied a disregard of the existing customs within the congregation, a failure to adapt to the given situation, and the danger of legalism. (He had uttered similar warnings in earlier letters: *WA* Br. 3, 373; 4, 40.)

[62] *WA* 12, 214.

worship. In order to prevent confusion, he called for conformity among churches of the same region,[63] and for a consistent observance of the order once it had been adopted.[64] His principle of love and regard for the common man made him the sworn enemy of arbitrary changes. In fact, he favored a wider degree of uniformity, as long as evangelical freedom could be maintained.[65]

Luther's directions for the observance of stated times and places conforms with these general ideas. Elsewhere we discussed his view of the sabbath rest and stressed that, far from being bound to certain days, it is a basic attitude of faith. But as a ceremonial law which appoints a certain day for worship, the Third Commandment is of no concern for the Christian.[66] But this does not preclude stated days of worship, when the Word can be heard and the Sacrament received. Under the conditions of this earthly life, the church needs holy days to gather all her people.[67] Sunday as the traditional day of worship may be observed in freedom, but not in a legalistic way, as though no service could be held on any other day, or as though the Christian conscience should be bound to any special date.[68]

By the same token, Luther was willing to retain the church year.[69] He pointed out that Christian truth cannot be parceled out among the various festival days. Easter, for example, is kept whenever we receive Holy Communion.[70] Of course, all the

[63] *WA* 19, 73.

[64] *WA* 19, 17; 49, 591.

[65] *WA* 54, 165; 50, 614.

[66] *WA* 16, 478 (Aurifaber); 18, 77; 49, 591 (print).

[67] *WA* 40 I, 624; 2, 540.

[68] *WA* 49, 592 (print); 40 I, 623; 50, 554.

[69] *WA* 12, 208; 19, 79.

[70] *WA* 31 I, 397. On the other hand, it must be said that the message in its entirety cannot receive its due on any single day but ought to be distributed over the course of the church year. See, for example, 45, 324 (Roerer).

saints' days which were not in accord with the gospel had to be discontinued. But Luther was willing to retain other special days, though he would have preferred to have their message proclaimed on the next Sunday.[71]

Closely related to these thoughts is Luther's picture of the church as a building. No place is sacred, except by the presence of God and his Word.[72] Properly speaking, the "temple" is not a building, but the presence of God. A Christian need not depend on sacred spots and places, for Christ is present everywhere and, as Christ told the Samaritan woman, can be worshiped anywhere.[73] In this life indeed we need definite places of worship. But Luther insisted that the conscience should not be bound to certain buildings and so be bereft of its Christian freedom.

A church is built in order to have the Word proclaimed and the sacraments administered. This is what the pulpit and altar are for, although the Word can also be preached without benefit of a pulpit, and the Supper received without an altar.[74] Luther found it impossible to conceive of an act of consecration which would set apart certain places and spots from the rest of creation. For their sacredness rests entirely on that of the Word and the Sacrament, and where these are received in faith, the place itself, even without any act of consecration, becomes a holy place.[75] Properly speaking, every place is sacred, because Christ

[71] *WA* 12, 37, 209.
[72] *WA* 10 I, 1, 384; 31 I, 179.
[73] *WA* 11, 444; 8, 470; 18, 211.
[74] *WA* 18, 211; 31 I, 406; 42, 72; 50, 649. The thesis of H. Preuss, "The altar corresponds to the Lutheran Supper, and the table to the Reformed" is not supported by the references from Luther which he quotes in *Der Altar des Sakraments* (1941), p. 224ff. Rather, Luther's attitude is marked by freedom. This basic view is not contradicted by his appreciation of ecclesiastical art, etc. See also 19, 80 where Luther expressed the wish to have the officiant stand behind the altar table and face the congregation.
[75] *WA* 49, 588 (print).

is present everywhere. But some places are especially sanctified by being used for holy things and by holy people. The finest cathedral is profaned if Christ fails to find an entrance into the hearts of men.[76] That is why Luther rejected the exclusive use of consecrated ground for worship in the Roman church.[77] It is not the ground (a good creation of God) that needs to be hallowed, but the men who go to worship there.[78]

Thus Luther subjected all the means that serve to enrich worship to the freedom of faith and the order of love. An early passage of his refers to a symbolic theology (*simbolica theologia*), a theology which would lead to God by way of symbolic action, art, and music.[79] But the rich liturgical symbolism which marks the medieval expositions of the mass and the Eastern liturgies was not accepted by him. To him the way of the gospel led through the ear more than the eye. That is why he valued poetry and music so highly, and the hymns which would sing the gospel into the hearts of the common people.[80] The Reformation caused a tremendous revival of the hymn. Luther solicited the help of poets and composers.[81] He himself became one of the greatest hymn writers the church has ever known and wrote for his hymns not only the words but also the tunes, and the music for the chants of the "German Mass." [82]

[76] *WA* 31 I, 179. [77] *WA* 18, 212.

[78] Cf. the same idea concerning the hallowing of the sabbath day in *WA* 38, 366.

[79] *WA* 57, 179 (Hb).

[80] *WA* 35, 474; 12, 218. Nevertheless Luther valued the Latin songs of the mass highly: See 30 II, 352.

[81] *WA* 12, 218; Br 3, 220 (to Spalatin).

[82] See the Introduction to Luther's hymns in *WA* 35, as well as Otto Schlisske, *Handbuch der Lutherlieder* (Goettingen: 1948); Th. Knolle, *Die Eucharistiefeier;* H. Preuss, *Martin Luther. Der Kuenstler* (Guetersloh: 1931), p. 89ff; Gerhard Kappner, *op. cit.,* p. 56ff; Paul Nettl, *Luther and Music* (Philadelphia: 1948).

The fine arts too he wished to have serve the gospel's cause. His fight against the Enthusiasts and Iconoclasts was a battle against all who would divorce the gospel from human culture.[83] Painting and architecture should be permitted, should indeed help to proclaim the Word. "It is better to paint on the wall how God created the world, how Noah built the ark, and other good stories . . . . Would to God I could persuade lords and rich people to have the whole Bible painted on houses inside and outside for everyone to see." [84] "He who wants an altar picture should have the Last Supper painted and with it the verse: 'He has made his wonderful works to be remembered: the Lord is gracious and full of compassion' written in large golden letters so that hearts should think of it and eyes should read it and thank and praise God. For as the altar is appointed for the Sacrament, no better picture could be appointed for it. The other pictures of God or Christ can be placed elsewhere." [85]

Vestments too might be used in freedom, as long as the gospel was preached. "About them [vestments] we feel as we do about other rites. We permit them to be used freely, but without pomp and luxury." [86] Without the gospel the finest pictures would be-

[83] *WA* 16, 437ff, 440f; 18, 67ff; 35, 475.

[84] *WA* 18, 82.

[85] *WA* 31 I, 415. It is questionable, however, whether Luther should be considered an artist as in the book by Preuss on Luther as an artist.

[86] *WA* 12, 214. Cf. 19, 80. In his famous letter to Probst C. Buchholzer in Berlin about external rites (Dec. 4, 1539, *WA* Br 8, 625), after stating his condition that the gospel be given free course, Luther adds these jocular remarks: "Thus you will be free to have a procession in the name of God, carry a silver or golden cross, and wear a chasuble or surplice of velvet, silk, or linen. If your lord the elector is not content with one chasuble or surplice, put on three of them as did Aaron the high priest . . . and if your electoral grace is not content with one procession in which you go around singing and ringing, then go around seven times, as did Joshua with the children of Israel, who made a noise and blew their trumpets. And if your lord the elector is so inclined, let him leap and dance in front with harps, drums, cymbals, and bells, as David did before the Ark of the Lord when it was brought to the city of

come a hypocrisy. Outwardly, God and the Saviour would be honored but actually they would be mocked, as by the Jews under the cross.[87]

It is only the abuse of these and other arts which the Word of God condemns. Believers are free to make use of them in the service of others. The only rule to be observed, besides liberty of conscience, is a certain moderation lest the devout be absorbed by external rights,[88] or place their trust in works of art which their liberality had procured for the church.[89] Churches ought to be built, pictures painted, and hymns composed in order to call men to the gospel, but not for men to do God a favor. And if ever the time should come when churchly ceremonial and pomp threaten the works of service and love, all the expenses for buildings, pictures, music, and the like would have to be deferred in favor of practical works of mercy.[90]

For as the one who freely gives and forgives, God is not bound to human rites and forms, sacred times and buildings, music and fine arts. As the Sovereign, he, and not man, decides when the Spirit will grip the heart of man.[91] All our liturgical arts and forms, all our attempts to draw men into the orbit of Christ must therefore not be allowed to obscure the one who himself is both the subject and object of worship: Jesus Christ. For Christ is God's service for us as well as our worship in faith. We will conclude

Jerusalem. I am well content with it, for such matters, as long as they are not abused, do not add to or take anything from the gospel. But they must not be made a matter of necessity for salvation, to constrain the conscience." Vestments and other liturgical helps should not be consecrated as though the consecration imparted a certain holiness to them, but should only be used with prayer and the Word of God (*WA* 12, 215).

[87] *WA* 11, 444.

[88] *WA* 6, 44; 50, 619, 651; 30 II, 349; 50, 670ff; 30 II, 604.

[89] *WA* 23, 508.

[90] *WA* 10 I, 2, 40, 80; 6, 45.

[91] Prenter, *op. cit.*, p. 249f, 256ff.

this study of worship with a passage by Luther which sets forth the Christian mass in its fullest meaning:

"Thank God, in our churches we are able to exhibit to a Christian the true Christian mass, according to the command and institution of Christ and in accordance with the sense of Christ and the church. Here comes to the altar our minister, bishop, or parish pastor who was rightly, openly, and publicly called and who before by baptism was consecrated, anointed, and born again a priest of Christ that needs no sectarian unction [*Winkel Cresem*]. Clearly and publicly, he chants the Words of Institution, takes bread and wine, gives thanks, and imparts them to us who are waiting to commune by virtue of the word of Christ: 'This is my body. This is my blood. This do, etc.' And we, that is, those who want to commune, are kneeling there beside, behind, and around him, men and women, young and old, master and servant, mistress and maid, parent and children, gathered by God, all of us true and holy co-priests, sanctified by the blood of Christ and by baptism anointed and consecrated. Here we are in our indigenous, hereditary, priestly honor and ornament, have (as described in Rev. 4) our golden crowns on our heads, harps in our hands, and golden vials full of incense, and we have our pastor proclaim the Word of Christ, but not for himself or for his own person. He is the mouthpiece for all of us, and in our hearts and with steadfast faith we all, with him, address the Lamb who is for us and with us and gives us his body and blood according to his own institution. This is our mass, the true mass which will never fail us."[92]

[92] *WA* 38, 247.

BIBLIOGRAPHY

AULEN, GUSTAV. *Christus Victor.* An Historical Study of the Three Main Types of the Idea of the Atonement. New York: Macmillan, 1951.

BAILLE, DONALD, and JOHN MARSH (eds.). *Intercommunion.* New York: Harper, 1952.

BRILIOTH, YNGVE. *Eucharistic Faith and Practice, Evangelical and Catholic.* New York: Macmillan, 1931.

DRURY, T. W. *Elevation in the Eucharist, its History and Rationale.* Cambridge, England: 1907.

EDWALL, PEHR, ERIC HAYMAN, W. D. MAXWELL (eds.). *Ways of Worship.* The Report of a Theological Commission on Faith and Order. New York: Harper, 1951.

HOEK, GOESTA. "Luthers lara om kyrkans aembete." English translation in *Scottish Journal of Theology,* I (1954), p. 16ff.

JOSEFSON, RUBEN. *Luther on Baptism.* Hongkong: 1952.

KRAMM, H. H. *The Theology of Martin Luther.* London: 1947.

NETTL, PAUL. *Luther and Music.* Philadelphia: Muhlenberg, 1948.

NYGREN, ANDERS. *Agape and Eros.* Philadelphia: Westminster, 1953.

——— (ed.). *This Is the Church.* Philadelphia: Muhlenberg, 1952.

STONE, DARWELL. *A History of the Doctrine of the Holy Eucharist.* Vol. I-II. London: 1909.

WINGREN, GUSTAF. *Luther on Vocation.* Philadelphia: Muhlenberg, 1957.

For a detailed bibliography of Scandinavian and German literature, cf. Vilmos Vajta, *Die Theologie des Gottesdienstes bei Luther* (Goettingen: Vandenhoeck, 1954), pp. 361-372.

INDEXES

SUBJECTS

Agnus Dei, 30
Alloiosis, 105
Altar, 184
Anamnesis. *See* Remembrance
Antichrist, 112
Apostle, 77, 80, 115, 150
Apostolic Succession. *See* Succession, apostolic
Art, 186f
Article, First, 86, 94, 106, 135
  Third, 148
Asceticism, 153
Atheism, 6
Atonement, 72f

Baptism, 3, 103, 112, 118f, 151, 154, 167f
Benedictus, 45
Beneficium, 26, 33f
Biblicism, 179

Calling, 166ff
Call, 111, 113ff
Canon law, 29, 147, 173
Canon of mass. *See* Mass, canon of
Catechism, Large, 4, 12
  Small, 148
Ceremonies, 172ff, 187
Character indelebilis, 120
Chorales, 161
Church, 20, 24, 139ff
Church building, 184
Church year, 183
Church, Orthodox, 32
Clergy, 99f, 111
Collect, 167
Commandment, First, 3, 10, 128
  Third, 130ff, 183
Communicatio idiomatum, 105
Communion, 42, 101, 135f
Confession of Praise. *See* Praise, Confession of
  of Sin. *See* Sin, Confession of
Congregation, 114ff
Conscience, 29, 34, 86, 138, 173, 178, 184, 187
Consecration, 98ff, 106, 184, 187
Conservativism, 174, 181ff
Consubstantiation, 95
Co-operation, 112f
Covenant, 40f
Creation, 7f, 12, 34, 61, 87f, 91, 94, 97, 105ff, 137
Credo, 30
Cross, 9, 59, 168ff
Culture, 186
Decalogue, 4
Deism, 97
Deus absconditus, 11, 14, 68, 87, 89, 91, 158
  cultus, 14f
  nudus, 15
  oblatus, 15
  pro nobis, 10, 19, 89
  praedicatus, 14
  revelatus, 14, 68

Devil, 8f, 13, 17, 73ff, 83, 87f, 97, 119, 126, 131, 142
Devotion, 60, 161f, 165
Diaconate, 120
Distribution, 53
Dualism, 11f, 20, 25, 141f

Elements, 42, 44, 97, 102
Elevation, 44f, 167
Enthusiasts, 28f, 71, 88f, 91, 97f, 102ff, 116, 128, 135, 139f, 166, 168, 173, 176
Episcopate, 114, 117, 121, 151
Eucharist. *See* Supper, Lord's
Exinanitio, 153
Externals, 15, 17, 23, 29f, 76, 88, 99, 116, 128, 134, 139, 172

Fear, 36
Flesh, 131, 136
Forgiveness, 35, 45, 101f, 112
Form. *See* Order
Freedom, 29, 171ff, 177ff, 187
Free will. *See* Will, free

Ghost, Holy, 70ff, 73, 86, 88, 93, 99, 116, 127, 148, 154, 158
Gift. *See Beneficium*
Gloria in Excelsis, 30
Gospel, 12, 31, 74, 79f, 83, 93, 120, 154, 158
Grace, 49, 61, 113, 145
Grace, means of, 15, 59, 110, 127, 139f

Habitus, 8, 128
Heaven, 86ff, 97f, 131
Heresy, 76f
History, redemptive, 79
Holiness, 129f
Host, 96
Host, adoration of, 101
Housefather, 117f
Humiliation, 153
Hymns, 161, 185, 187

Iconoclasts, 186
Idolatry, 3-18, 25, 30, 129, 142, 145
Imitation, 79
Incarnation, 15, 19, 25, 41, 68f, 87, 97, 105
Intercession, 165f
Interpretation, 76ff, 81

Justification, 50, 78, 129

Keys, power of, 112
Kingdoms, two, 110f

Laity, 111, 118
  cup for, 52f
Larvae, 116
Law, 9, 12, 38, 40, 54f, 74, 79f, 83, 87, 152f, 158
Law, ceremonial, 29, 177ff
Legalism, 79, 178f, 183
Liberty. *See* Freedom
Light, inner, 71, 76
Litany, 165
Lord's Supper. *See* Supper, Lord's
Love, 14, 34, 74, 167, 171ff, 174ff, 177ff, 187

Manducatio infidelium, 134, 143
Mass, canon of, 29ff, 52, 60ff, 102, 136, 165
Mass, use of, 46ff
Mass, private, 51, 53, 161f
Mass, sacrifice of, 27ff, 38ff, 45f, 53ff, 71, 96, 99, 113, 119, 181
Mass, votive, 32, 167
Means of Grace. *See* Grace
Meditation, 76
Mercy, 33ff, 87
Merit, 47, 72, 81, 145
Ministry, 109ff
  of women, 117
Monasticism, 9, 32, 37, 157, 166f
Mortification, 152, 175
Music. *See* Chorales, Hymns, Song
Mysticism, 130, 171

Neo-Protestantism, 16, 24
Nominalism, 56

Offense, 92
Offertory, 166f
Office, 81
Omnipotence, 89f, 96ff
Omnipresence, 85ff, 95ff, 104
Opus operantis, 46ff
Opus operatum, 17, 38, 46ff, 92, 152, 173
Order, 29, 171ff
  pliancy of, 177ff
Ordinary, 30
Ordination, 113ff

Paintings. *See* Art
Passivity, 128ff, 174
Pericopes, 75, 81

Philology, 76
Philosophy, 94f, 97
Pledge, 42, 99
Praise, confession of, 157ff
  sacrifice of, 21, 24, 151f, 154ff
Prayer, 144, 161ff
Prayer, Lord's, 104, 144, 164ff
Preaching, 16f, 67ff, 112, 119ff, 133ff, 158f, 176
Predestination, 11, 14, 148
Presence, real, 91ff, 96ff
Pride, 13, 157
Priesthood, 54f, 115ff, 118, 128f, 149ff, 166. *See also* Clergy
Promise, 40f, 46, 162
Psychology, 126, 133

Reason, 7, 94, 157
Reconciliation, 34, 74
Redemption, 72ff, 89, 96, 103, 106f, 130
Remembrance, 57f, 60, 83, 97f, 136
Repentance, 158
Repraesentatio, 57f
Revelation, 17, 19, 68f, 91ff
Righteousness. *See* Justification
Rites, 172ff

Sabbath, 130ff, 183, 185
Sacrament, 16, 19ff, 24, 42, 47, 91, 119, 134
  adoration of, 160f
Sacrifice, 38, 54ff, 149ff. *See also* Mass, Prayer, Praise, Thanksgiving
Saints, adoration of, 9, 81
Sanctification, 130
Sanctus, 30, 44
Scholasticism, 8, 46ff, 55, 93ff
Scripture, 67ff, 75ff
Self-accusation, 157f
Self-communion, 53f
Sermon. *See* Preaching
Sign, 16, 45, 92ff, 98f, 102
Sin, confession of, 157ff
Song, 156, 158
Speculation, 98
Spirit. *See* Ghost, Holy
Spiritual, 87f
Stewardship, 166f
Succession, apostolic, 110, 118
Supper, Lord's, 3, 27ff, 85ff, 119, 160f
  institution of, 27ff, 39ff, 51ff, 82, 99ff
Symbols, 98, 185

Temptation, 138
Testamentum, 38ff, 100
Thanksgiving, 21, 23, 60, 152, 154ff
Tongues, 81
Traditions, human, 32, 179
Transubstantiation, 53, 90, 93ff, 99, 110

Ubiquity, 86
Uniformity, 182

Vestments, 186

Warfare, spiritual, 13f, 69, 73ff, 78ff, 88, 141
Will, free, 14f
Women. *See* Ministry
Word, 3, 16f, 21, 24, 67ff, 73ff, 85ff, 90ff, 99
Work, daily, 14
Work of God, 16, 70ff, 90
Work righteousness, 9, 13, 17f, 46ff, 50f, 57f, 156ff
Wrath, 7ff, 13, 33f, 73f, 80, 87

NAMES

Allwohn, xi, 14, 24, 69, 180
Althaus, 20, 99, 103
Altmann, 118
Aristotle, 94f
Askmark, 110, 120
Asmussen, 91
Augustine, 100, 151
Aulen, 8, 54, 73, 139, 141

Baillie, ix
Barge, 180
Barth, 77, 91, 98, 135
Behm, 40
Benktson, 77, 98
Bergendoff, 110
Biel, 57
Bohlin, 107, 169
Bornkamm, 6
Brilioth, ix, 39f, 42, 52, 80f, 95, 168, 181
Bring, 8, 20, 34, 42f, 54, 96, 98, 126, 136, 140, 156
Browe, 44
Brunner, ix, 154, 172
Buehler, 138

Chrysostom, 39

Degering, 57
Dietz, xi
Dittrich, 131, 164
Drews, 118, 120
Drury, 44

Eck, 39
Edwall, ix
Eger, 168
Elert, 111, 115
Ellwein, 132

Fagerberg, 114, 142
Fendt, 22, 28, 52, 125, 131, 162, 182
Feuerbach, 5
Flemming, x, xi, 17, 20, 22, 23, 172
Fransen, 180
Franz, 32, 44, 52
Frey, 129

Gennrich, 86, 91, 93, 95, 98
Gogarten, 6
Gollwitzer, 16, 91, 94f, 102f
Gottschick, 20, 28, 125, 181
Graebke, 43
Graff, ix, 181
Gregory the Great, 32
Guehloff, 157

Haar, 128
Harbsmeier, 17
Hardeland, 131
Hayman, ix
Heckel, 173
Heiler, 28
Hermann, 128
Hirsch, 11
Hoek, 110, 150
Holl, x, 14, 16, 24, 36f, 80, 120

Iserloh, 57, 59
Iwand, 126

Jacobs, 4
Jacoby, 20, 125
Joest, 128, 131
Johannesson, 86, 145
Josefson, 110, 114, 120, 154, 157
Jungmann, 44, 167

Kant, 11
Kappner, 59, 165, 185
Karlstadt, 92, 97
Kattenbusch, 11
Kittel, 40
Knolle, 25, 83, 101, 172, 185

Koenker, ix
Kramm, 110, 119

Lerfeldt, 164
Lilje, 107
Lind, 165
Lindberg, 80
Lindroth, 120
Ljunggren, 6, 93, 102f, 131, 153
Loewenich, 164

Marsh, ix
Maurer, 171, 181
Maxwell, ix
Melanchthon, 103
Mensching, ix, 20
Meyer, 131
Molland, x
Moses, 36, 79, 149

Nettl, 148
Nygren, 20, 92, 106, 114, 120, 137, 140, 150, 174

Olsson, 6, 92, 140f, 141, 143, 153, 168, 171f, 174ff

Prenter, 7, 16, 68, 76, 81, 93, 103, 137, 148, 154, 158, 176
Preuss, 184ff

Reed, x
Rendtorff, 30
Renz, ix, 57
Rietschel, 17, 21, 114, 118, 120, 181
Runestam, 171f, 175f

Sasse, 91
Scheel, 36
Schifferdecker, 168
Schleiermacher, 22, 103
Schlink, 140
Schlisske, 185
Schmidt, 58
Schott, 129, 157
Seeberg, E., 11, 68
Seeberg, R., 11, 47, 82, 95
Smend, 52
Sohm, 139ff
Sommerlath, 91, 98, 100, 102f, 136
Staehlin, ix, xi
Stange, 102, 168
Stone, ix, 57
Strodach, x

Thieme, 68, 166
Thomas, 151, 160
Thomas Aquinas, 57

Vossberg, 12, 18

Widding, 23
Wingren, 6, 69, 72, 111f, 131, 133, 137, 145, 168f, 171f, 174, 178

Zwingli, 135

SCRIPTURE QUOTATIONS

Gen. 1 48
Gen. 4:41 50

Lev. 26:36 86

II Kings 16:10ff 31

Ps. 18:25f 143
Ps. 50:12-14 156
Ps. 50:23 159
Ps. 102:21 82
Ps. 111:4f 82f
Ps. 139:7f 85

Isa. 55:11 141
Isa. 66:1 85

Jer. 23:23 85

Matt. 8:13 10
Matt. 12:1-8 143
Matt. 17:5 68
Matt. 17:25ff 177
Matt. 18:19 117
Matt. 18:10 90
Matt. 28:20 90

Luke 10:42 67
Luke 17:11-19 155
Luke 22:19 82, 97
Luke 24:30ff 22

John 1:1 69
John 4:23 160
John 6 104

Acts 17:27 85

Rom. 1:23 9
Rom. 3:25 143
Rom. 10:17 132f
Rom. 12:1 151f
Rom. 14:1 177
Rom. 15:16 159

I Cor. 9:20 177
I Cor. 11:26 60, 82, 97

Gal. 2:14f 132
Gal. 2:20 54, 129
Gal. 3:13 72
Gal. 3:15 40
Gal. 3:18 41
Gal. 6:14 132

Eph. 4 144

Phil. 2:5ff 153

Col. 2:9 102

Titus 1:5 115f

Heb. 6:6 55
Heb. 7:12 149
Heb. 7:27 56
Heb. 9:13ff 39
Heb. 9:16 41
Heb. 10:11ff 56
Heb. 13:15 151

James 80

I Pet. 2:5 50, 151, 159
I Pet. 2:9 150f

Rev. 1:6 150
Rev. 4 188
Rev. 5:10 150
Rev. 20:6 150